D0604006

PICKUPS

★ A LOVE STORY ★

All photography by Howard Zehr except where noted.
Photos page 92 by Wade Bowman, page 136 courtesy
Brandon Derrow, page 208 by Steven D. Johnson.

Design by Cliff Snyder

PICKUPS: A LOVE STORY
Copyright © 2013 by Good Books, Intercourse, PA 17534
International Standard Book Number: 978-1-56148-788-2
Library of Congress Control Number: 2013934684

All rights reserved. Printed in the United States of America.
No part of this book may be reproduced in any manner, except
for brief quotations in critical articles or reviews, without permission.

Publisher's Cataloging-in-Publication Data
Zehr, Howard.
    Pickups : a love story , pickup trucks , their owners , their stories /
Howard Zehr.
        p. cm.
        ISBN 978-1-56148-788-2
    1. Pickup trucks. 2. Pickup trucks --Pictorial works. 3. Trucks. I. Title.

TL230.5.P49 Z44 2013
629.223/2 --dc23   2013934684

Pickup Trucks,
Their Owners, Their Stories

HOWARD ZEHR

Good Books
Intercourse, PA 17534
800/762-7171
www.GoodBooks.com

TABLE OF CONTENTS

About this Book   7

ABOUT THIS BOOK

This book contains photographs of an array of pickup trucks—vintage and modern, junkers and show trucks, hot rods and work trucks, standard and customized. But this is also a book about people and their personal identities, their relationships, their pasts as well as their presents. It is a book of stories and reflections.

These pickup owners have relationships with their trucks. Mostly they are relationships of affection, but a few are ambivalent. For some they are working or recreational relationships, while for others they are relationships of admiration, memory, and preservation. For many they are relationships that reflect or help define their personal identities and even provide the means of self-expression. For some, they are a connection to a lost past or a marker of a specific stage in life.

Pickups and their associated activities are often a family affair. Trucks also provide connections to a larger community of people, a way to make and maintain friendships, and even access to a community of knowledge. And for a few, their pickups are symbols of romantic or marriage relationships.

This is a book about love—love not just of trucks but of people as well.

I confess I didn't quite suspect all of this when I started the project. I like trucks, and I knew that trucks mattered to my fellow Virginians. Little did I realize the many layers of meaning that would unravel.

And, yes, all of these trucks are from Virginia, the state in which I live.

The project began when Merle Good, one of my publishers, casually asked, "Why don't you do a book about people and their pickup trucks?" I didn't know if he was serious, but at the time I was preoccupied with a cycle of heavy photography and interview books about life-sentenced prisoners, victims of violent crime, and children whose parents were in prison. Several years later, though, I was ready for something lighter. It turned out that Merle was serious; when I proposed this book, Merle and Phyllis Good immediately scheduled it for publication—and I hadn't started yet.

I'm a bit of an introvert, so I had to screw up my courage to reach out to strangers with my odd request. Once I began, however, I could hardly stop seeking out trucks and owners, looking at their trucks, hearing their stories. Even though the book is finished, I'm still tempted to chase down interesting trucks. The trucks were fascinating, but so were the people and their stories and reflections. It has been a privilege to have an excuse to meet and listen to the people in this book.

As my friend, Mark Metzler Sawin, reflects in the closing essay, in American culture our vehicles often say something about who we are. They provide keys to identity, serve as repositories of memories, and often function as forms of self-expression. For me, there was my first car—a two-tone 1955 Chevy V8. I patched the rust spots, worked on the mechanics, dated my first real girlfriend with it, and proudly took it cruising around Bower's Drive-In, the happening place for teenagers in Goshen, Indiana, in the late '50s and early '60s. The VW bug that my wife and I drove when we were married in the 1960s also carries many memories.

But pickup trucks seem to have a special place in our hearts, and that isn't true only for men. Debbie Snyder, who probably sells more pickups than any other dealer in our area, says that women are at least as attached to their trucks as men—and maybe more. My wife, Ruby, loved the rusty Toyota pickup that she used for her garden design business and mourned when we had to part with it.

Although some professions obviously require pickups, attachment to trucks doesn't necessarily follow professional lines. I did not identify all the truck owners' professions, but they include doctors, farmers, lawyers, contractors, airline pilots, musicians, and more.

This selection of people and stories is not a scientific sample and so is not fully representative of the trucks found in Virginia. There are more older trucks in this book than very new ones, for example; new trucks don't carry the stories and depth of relationship that older ones do.

I went looking for interesting trucks, trucks with interesting stories, and people who were passionate about their trucks. I asked around, following leads that people gave me. I contacted car and truck clubs, attended cruise-ins and vintage vehicle shows. I "stalked" interesting trucks, following them until I got a chance to talk with their owners or to put a card about the project on their windshields. (I cherish an

"Instead of photography as taking, we can envision it as receiving. Instead of a trophy that is hunted, an image is a gift."
— From *The Little Book of Contemplative Photography*

image of my friend, Mark, wildly trying to flag down a woman driving a big black truck with pink trim. She waved dubiously at this happy but suspicious man and drove on.) Generous people such as Patty and Bob Metcalfe and "Doc" Art Carter took it upon themselves to organize visits for me with pickup owners in their communities.

In the end, I had more stories and trucks than we were able to include. My apologies to those who were not included. It was not that they weren't worthy. It was a matter of space and balance.

I am grateful to all the pickup owners who shared their stories and trucks with me and for the many who suggested leads or ideas for the project. Mark Metzler Sawin, whose essay concludes this book, served as a sounding board and encouraged me in various ways. A special thanks to Merle, Phyllis, and Kate Good, who encouraged the project and saw it through publication, to Jo Fisher, who was the final editor, and to Cliff Snyder, who designed it. Thanks also to Jim Christian, who invited me to be a beta tester for his new PhotoNinja software. The images in this book were captured in Nikon's RAW format and converted with this outstanding RAW converter.

A project like this is never a one-person effort, and I am grateful for the many contributions of others.

— *Howard Zehr*

GEORGE AND KATHY DUKE

It's taking something that looks dead and lost and bringing it back to life.

GEORGE: It's a 1931 Ford Model A closed cab pickup. Henry Ford would make running changes on cars as the year went along—whatever he thought was better. He contracted with the Budd Wheel Company to build an all-steel closed cab. This is one of the very first. Before this, most vehicles had a cloth insert. And in August of that year, they went to a wider bed on the back. So this truck is referred to as a wide bed, steel top pickup truck—a very late '31. The truck was made in Norfolk, Virginia.

I've had it fifty years in June. I bought it in '63, the year I got out of high school. It had been disassembled by a kid who wanted to build a hot rod. A friend and I brought it home in card-

board boxes and old wooden bushel baskets with wire handles. I worked on it while I was in college. I was never a good student, so I'd study as long as I could stand it. Then I'd go to the garage and wire brush something and paint it. It probably took me ten years before I got it together.

I was driving it one day shortly after I put it together and had some friends sitting in the bed in the back. The left wheel came off and passed by us. Everybody got scared, but nobody got hurt.

In the early '80s I was in the insulation busi-ness. The economy went south, and one of my suppliers put me into involuntary bankruptcy. I was afraid I was going

to lose everything. I took the pickup apart so when they came to look at it, they wouldn't think it had any value. Then I put it back together in the late '80s. At that time I had it painted, and then I restored it. I'm the purist, so I kept it all original. The biggest thing to me is taking something that looks dead and lost and bringing it back to life.

When Kathy and I first met about twenty-five years ago, one of our first dates was in an old pickup truck—carrying stuff to the dump.

KATHY: He knew if I did that, I was okay! When I met him, he had a Model A, and I had a '65 Mustang. I have always been interested in old vehicles. He's definitely the mechanic.

I know a lot about 'em and can fiddle with them, but I'm not a mechanic.

We love to tour. And our grandchildren and neighbors like to pile in and ride around. We take kids to the ice cream store in it. It's rural where we are, and we take them to a certain point. Once we get to the sheriff's house, we stop! But the sheriff got arrested, so he was doing a lot worse than we're doing.

It's a fun hobby. The other people in it are good, too.

BARRY CARPENTER

> *The more rust you have,*
> *the prouder you can be about it.*

We have three and a half acres, and it seems like there is always something that needs to be done that we can't do in a car. So in 1990 we found this used 1985 F-150 long-bed pickup with a manual shift and a V6. It worked fine, but it had this farmer smell in it. I didn't really pay much attention to it, but my kids said, "Man, what's up?" So I had to get some Clorox and clean it out. It still was not beautiful, but it passed their test.

It's not a full-time farm truck. It's more of a "when you need it" kind of truck. I don't take it out on the road a lot. Its main job is to haul debris from projects, to bring stuff home that I buy, and to take things to the dump. We call her Brown Beauty.

It's kinda deteriorating. I was standing up against the front of it the other day, talking on the cell phone, and I bumped the medallion. It fell off. Things are falling off all the time. About a year and a half ago,

I was going to the brush dump. I was going down one of the back roads and had to cross some railroad tracks. I heard something go, "Kaboom! Boom!" I kept going up the road, crested a hill, and I heard another bump. I slowed down and looked out my side window, and my spare tire was rolling down the hill ahead of me. I had to stop and run and chase down the tire.

One thing I'll tell you about the truck: I'm totally incognito in it. I'm not a land planner. I'm not from someplace else. I'm just a guy in a truck. There's a whole camaraderie with others in their trucks. The more rust you have, probably, the prouder you can be about it—up to a certain point.

When the kids were in their teens, we would take the truck and ride around the field, before they could legally drive. They loved it, just loved it. My son brought the grandkids up awhile back, and we got

the grandson in the truck. He didn't drive it—he's only 5—but he loved it. So it's kinda like, "Let's keep that truck around for the kids." It's definitely part of the family. I fully expect to have my grandson and granddaughter out in the field, driving around.

The story on Patches—the cat—is that he showed up one day. He became my best buddy. He followed me everywhere. He's like a puppy dog. Every time I'd go to the truck, he'd get up on the back, walk along the side of the bed, climb up, and then look in the back window at me. If ever I left the window open, he'd be in the truck. I've got pictures of him sitting in the driver's seat. He can't reach the pedals, but he can shift! He's a great cat, and he loves being out there.

A few years ago I started taking oil painting classes. I was thinking, "What can I paint out in the backyard?" So I painted the truck.

KELLY RANDOLPH

Trucks are my thing.

Any trucks I've owned, I've always fixed them up. I've completely redone the '51 Ford. Safety features, brake lights, turn signals—all customized. I go in spurts. I fool with a truck a little bit, then I won't do anything for a little bit, then I'll go back to it.

My daddy, my uncles, and my granddad always had trucks growing up. My uncle had a friend who had a '56 Ford pickup. He had a Thrush muffler on that. I used to ride with my dad, and I was hooked. When I had an opportunity to get this one, I jumped on it.

Now I have three trucks, so, yeah, trucks are my thing. I'm gonna spend my money on something. Earlier it was

Duke Randolph (Kelly's father), Kelly, and Richard Randolph

bills, bills, bills. Over the years, I got raises and saved my money, so everything's paid. Now I put my money into my trucks and helping my sons.

Both of my boys love shows. People wave and check out the truck — they're in heaven. Shows

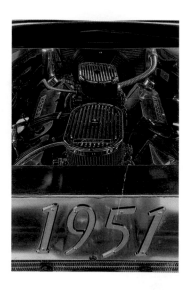

are good because you hang out with family. You can meet people, talk to different people.

The white truck is a 2000 Ford F-250 Super Duty with a nine-inch lift kit and V10 motor. There are blue neon lights that light up the whole underneath, and the whole inside wheel well is red. And it has a boomin', boomin' stereo system.

Its bumper height is right at the Virginia legal limit — twenty-nine and

a half inches. This is basic compared to some of the trucks I've seen. Other than the lift kit and the lights, it's still a regular truck. It doesn't go on dirt roads, though, because there's so much cleaning, especially underneath. Usually if I'm going to a show, I start cleaning it on a Wednesday, takin' my time.

Uncle Richard had dump trucks and trailer trucks ever since we were kids. We could hear him comin' down the road. The road turned to dirt for maybe half a mile. If we were riding with him, he'd get out on the gas tank and let us drive. We were hooked, when we were kids, on big trucks.

Uncle Richard also had swans. Then I had an uncle from D.C. who had a Cadillac with a swan on it that lit up. I'm like, "Oh, man, that's cool." When I was in the shop, there was one in the case for twenty-some bucks. So I had to jump on that.

The Dodge—it's mainly for work and snow. I had an Acura TL, which was perfectly good, but it just was no good in the snow. It snowed one day when I was going to work, and I couldn't get off my street. I said, "As soon as I get home from work, I'm gettin' online. There's no way I'm gonna miss work because of my car."

Women like the blue one best. The young, young girls like the white one. But when I get to a show, when they have the Women's Choice—which is a special award—I've won every single time with the blue one. They like it for some reason. They say it's cute. Last week, coming through town, I was sitting at a red light, and several women were freakin' out, taking pictures. Yeah, women like it.

I'm never finished with these trucks. I always see something to change or something breaks, so I'm constantly foolin' with them.

BUCK CUNNINGHAM

It's a mixed breed.

It all started with that door. I had a piece of a 1950 truck for twenty-five years. We weren't gonna work on it 'til we had a door. Then a friend gave me that door, and I went to work. A big tree had come right up through the truck. I had to saw that tree down.

The gas pedal came off of one of my wife's sewing machines. She'd kill me if she found out I was robbing parts from that to build this truck. The hood cover over the transmission is from a Craftsman lawnmower. I was up at the junkyard one day, and I said, "Man

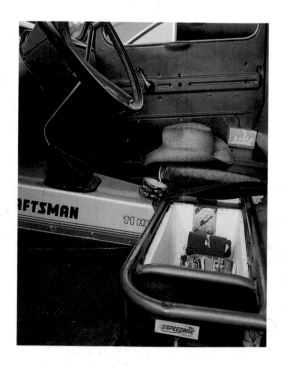

that hood—I believe it'll fit over top of this transmission." I carried it home, and it works in there like a top. The fender, that's a molasses barrel. I cut it right in half.

That's a Camaro frame front part. I tied onto it with channel flat tubing. It's got a Chevrolet steering box and a Ford power steering pump. The differential came out of a '70 Nova. The grill—that's a '79 Ford. The motor is from a 390 Ford pickup truck. These are '61 Cadillac taillights. The seatbelts are from an aircraft. I know they'll hold you in. So this is a mixed breed of every color.

There's the beer cooler. Back in my younger days, I hated totin' a cooler around, so I built the

The gas gauge

beer cooler up under the front seat.

I'm just a car nut—been all my life. I told my wife when I met her, "If you don't like cars, you don't like me, 'cause I'm a car nut." She hung with me. She'd get in the garage and help me pull transmissions out and everything else. But when she got older, she'd say, "When are you ever gonna grow up and quit messin' with them cars?" I said, "What did I tell you in '57? I ain't gonna never grow up." If you're a nut, you're a nut.

JOSH BACON

The kids like to pretend it's a boat and fish off the back.

When Darcy, my wife, was pregnant, we wanted something with four doors, so we got a Dodge Dakota 2002 with the double cab. It's got four doors and an extra long bed. I love it because I pick up things at the dump and along the side of the road. It sometimes drives my wife crazy, but that's one reason I love having a truck. It's my everyday car—to and from work, weekends, trips, everything.

It's got a major squeak in it, and it's gotten worse over the years. So I turn up the radio, and I don't even notice it anymore. My wife, when she drives it, she notices it and can't stand it. I

think I've just totally blocked it out. I've learned to live with it.

Our dogs ride in the back. All three of my girls love playing in the back. They like to pretend it's a boat and fish off the back. And they love having the dogs back there. I had a bloodhound for twelve years. His name was Blue. He was big and stinky and drooled, but he was the nicest, gentlest dog. He was so good with the kids. My memories of my truck are taking him up to Rawley Springs and fishing—just me and him.

What I love is when I ask my daughter, "If you could have any car in the world you want, what would it be?" and she says, "A green pickup." "No, no. I mean anything—a sports car, a convertible, a big truck." "No, I love this truck." I don't know how long that will last. She's 8 and a very tomboy type girl. She wears her hat backwards, lives in Broadway, and wants a pickup truck.

It suits my family so well. It can hold all my kids comfortably, and they can get in and out of the doors themselves. When we really pile peo-

ple in, there can be three on the back seat and three in the front. And then we still got the bed. It's the perfect size. I think I'll always have a pickup truck—I don't see that changing.

We got goats this past spring, and I went to get a goat hutch out in Hinton, in the middle of nowhere. It was an Amish farm-type store. I'm not a farmer, so when he showed me the goat house, it was huge. It's big and round and five feet high and has this big cone on the top. We put it in the back all awkwardly, and I asked the farmer, "Do you think I'll make it home?" The old farmer said, "I don't usually try to put things bigger than my truck in the back."

LUIS "CHEECH" PEREZ

I'm not a spring chicken anymore, so I needed a little more reliable transportation.

I never had a 4-wheel drive vehicle before I lost my leg in a motorcycle accident. I bought this one about two years ago. I'm gettin' up there. I'm not a spring chicken anymore, so I needed a little more reliable transportation. It's a nice, small truck—fits my needs. I don't haul a lot of big stuff around. And the motorcycle fits on the back if I really need to haul it anywhere. I'm still on the same bike I lost my leg on.

If I have nothing better to do and it's nice, I'll put in a good CD and cruise around, park by the beach. I sit in the back and listen to my stereo and kick back, watch the sunset, and just take in everything that goes on around here. It's multiple purpose; it does everything. If I want to sleep in it, I throw a mattress in the back. It's just practical. It's only me. I have no children, and I'm not married or anything. It suits my needs. I live a very humble life. I try to live as a good person and be trusting and honest with people and just go through the day.

SHANNON POLLOCK

> ## *Each thing that's wrong with it means it's something else I get to learn.*

I bought my truck on eBay when I was in a negotiation class. Our professor had us track negotiations that we were engaged in. I looked at what these trucks went for on eBay, and I could see there was a range from about $2,000 to $5,000—pretty pricey for a crappy truck. I decided that I wasn't going to go over $2,000. I'd just have to wait, and once prices went over that, I had to walk away from it. I ended up getting the truck for $2,000, but I did have to pay to have it shipped from Ohio.

It showed up and the driver's like, "I don't know if you knew

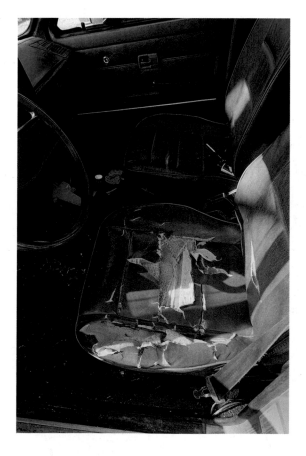

what you were getting." It wouldn't start so I was thinking, "Well, I guess I bought a truck that doesn't work." We rolled it by hand off of the trailer, and the guy drove off. There I was with my truck that wouldn't start.

I don't really know much about how cars work, but I wanted to learn about them, which is part of why I got the truck. So I looked under the hood, and it was really easy to tell right away—oh, the battery is not connected. So it was an easy first diagnosis.

I got the truck because I also wanted to make biodiesel. I really have no knowledge about trucks and biodiesel. I think the only thing to do is just start. To get it on the road, we took the lights apart and put new bulbs in the headlights that didn't work. That first jumping in—it was really exciting for my mom to see.

What I was originally thinking, besides the biodiesel business, was being able to put all my stuff in the back of a truck. It gives a lot of self-sufficiency and independence from everything. I have a little bit of paranoia about our society totally falling apart. If you have a biodiesel pickup, then it's another step in going off the grid because you can have transportation without depending on gasoline. All of that sentiment about freeing yourself from dependence on other things was part of what I was after, but it kinda turned into the opposite of that. Now I'm dependent on people who can help me fix my truck. But that's a good thing. It's been a really good learning experience to have to let people help me fix it.

I didn't get a hunting license this fall because I figured I was going to be in law school and I wouldn't have time. I

was a little bit disappointed about that. Then I was driving home from school one day on a motorcycle, and I saw this big buck walking across the road. The truck driver ahead of me didn't see it and ran smack into the buck.

I turned around on my bike and went back. This all happened in front of a campus police substation at the University of Virginia, so there was already an officer there. I asked him if he needed help with the deer, and he was like, "What d'ya mean? You have a firearm on you?"

"Nope. What I really meant is can I have it?" He said, "Sure, but how are you going to take it on your motorcycle?" I said, "Oh, I'll go home, get my truck, and come back."

It was really a funny experience. I was squatting there, gutting it. I've butchered a few deer, but I don't really know what I'm doing. But it has always been my dream to butcher a road-kill deer. I pretended to know what I was doing until it was kind of gutted. Then

when I was driving home, my truck kept cutting off. Finally it just wouldn't start again at all, so I called my neighbor, Wayne, to come and pick me up.

Wayne and I hung the deer from one of the trees in the yard. The deer was so heavy that Wayne tied a rope around its legs and threw the rope over the branch. We tied the other end of the rope onto Wayne's truck, and he slowly drove away while I bear-hugged the deer and lifted it up.

There was a law school fundraising ball that I was supposed to go to that night. We got the skin off the deer and got it thoroughly gutted and cleaned. But we ended up letting it hang over-night because I had to go and wash up and turn into a lady. The next morning we finished butchering it.

I don't know at this point if I'm more law school or redneck or something else. Being a girl driving a truck feels really cool. I feel like people see my piece of shit truck coming down the road, and I'm assuming they have assumptions about who I'm gonna be. I pull up, and it's a young girl who goes to law school—just not who you'd expect to be driving a truck. I

get a kick out of that—especially pulling up at the law school where everybody has their parents' fancy hand-me-down BMWs. To pull up in that truck in that parking lot, there's nothing that compares to it.

It rattles and shakes a lot when I drive it, especially idling at a traffic light. But if I kinda play with the gas and the clutch a little I can get to a place where it is smooth and stops rattling. I think that's kind of a fun thing about driving it. With the truck, I'm interacting with it when I drive. Each thing that's wrong with it means it's something else I get to learn.

Shannon and her mother, Alyce

ALYCE POLLOCK

The door is a badge of honor that says this vehicle is worth saving.

It's the truck of my husband's dreams. He signed a contract for his first real job, he signed a contract on a house, and the very next day he signed a contract on that truck.

It's the work truck, which means I drive it more than he does. It's the truck that we don't have to worry about getting messed up because it's already been messed. It hauls goats, chickens, lots of lumber, and lots and lots of garbage. Everybody has to have a pickup, and I really don't want a new pickup because then I'd be afraid I was gonna mess it up.

It's really funny because it's like I'm wearing a Halloween costume and I forget that I have this weird witch makeup or bald head thing going on. I forget that. When I'm inside the truck, I'm just a car driving down the road.

My opinion of what it means to have a different color door on my vehicle has changed. It used to

be like, "That's a real clunker. Why don't they at least paint it so it matches?" But now I think it says, "This vehicle is worth saving." It's badge of honor.

WOODY BROWN, JR.

I bought two and made one.

It's a '57. I bought two and made one. I bought one up in a holler. A boy told me the truck was back there, so we rode back and looked at the thing. The cab was shot. The bed was good. We walked around. I held my finger like, "Will you take $100?" And he said, "Yeah, that'd be good." And I asked, "Do you have a title?" "No, the title burned up in a guy's house some years ago, and he gave it to me." So the price of the truck just came down. I said, "Will you take $50 for it?" "Sure!"

I used the bed and the frame off of that. Then I bought the other one. I used the cab and fenders off of it. It had a 265

motor in it and the old granny 4-speed in it. It was all original—everything was there, even the old oil filter.

I ran it like that for probably three or four years, and then I decided I wanted to change things around. I bought a '70 Monte Carlo for $25. The boy wanted $400 for it. Every time I asked—$400. So one day I was riding with my friend, Jim, and we stopped at the boy's house. And Jim says, "Kenny, want a beer?" "Oh, yeah. I'll drink a beer." So he gave him a beer. He said, "Kenny, you take $25 for that piece of junk there?" And the boy said, "Yeah." So he turned around and said, "Woody, pay 'im."

I took the Monte Carlo and my pickup chassis, and I put the two frames together. I cut what I needed off the '57. Then I cut off the Monte Carlo and welded them together. I had the chassis sitting in the garage one day, and a fellow looked at it and says, "Did you measure to see if it was square?" I said, "No, I didn't." So we put a tape measure on it, and I was three quarters of an inch off. I couldn't believe it.

I put the motor in on the chassis and put the transmission in. Then I put the cab on and then the front end. The grill is original. That's one thing I wanted to keep original. I sat down in it one day and turned around, and I stepped down, and I didn't step any further. This thing is awful low! The underneath cross member on the chassis is barely off the road. So when I go up a gravel road, I can spread the gravel real easy.

I've had the truck on the road since '90. I have $4,600 in that truck, actual cash. My time working on it—you can't figure it, no way.

My next project is to change the cab because the floorboards are bad. That cab came off of a '58. When I put it back together, I'm probably going to put a bench seat in it to have a place for a third person. My daughter is probably going to end up with it. One of my grandsons wants it, but she says, "I may let you drive it, but you got to take my sons with you."

STEVEN "COBY" DEAN

A truck is everything you want.

It's my baby, oh yeah. I got this one because I've always wanted a bigger truck. As soon as I looked at this truck, I was like, "This is my truck." I got a job, and I can afford it now. I've wanted to spoil myself a little bit, give myself some incentives, so I just got rid of my old truck. I think a week ago it settled in, "You don't have your red truck no more." And I was like, "Ah, man. That was my first truck."

It's an '07, a Chevrolet. I think one of the reasons why I went Chevy is—you know Justin Moore, the country artist? He sings a song called "Bed of my Chevy." And that truck,

that same body style, was in Kip Moore's music video for "Somethin' 'Bout a Truck."

I pulled stuff with my old truck: cattle trailers, horse trailers, and trailers with hay on them. I made it do the job. I trusted it, I believed in it, and it did it. But it wasn't enough. This one here, I can pull trailers, and

> *Something about a truck in a field*
> *And a girl in a red sundress with an ice cold*
> *beer to her lips.*
> — from Kip Moore,
> "Somethin' 'Bout a Truck"

I can go anywhere I need to go. I can drive in a truck and feel like it looks good. I have a very big problem with driving a vehicle that doesn't look good. I want it to stick out, and this one sticks out.

I don't know if it looks like a redneck truck or not. What it says about me is this is my taste, and you can either like it or you can't—plain and simple. There's stuff I wanta put on that truck that people don't agree with. It's my truck to express myself—a statement, to be honest with you, to rub in everybody's faces. When I was in high school, there were people who didn't think I could make it, didn't think I would be anybody. It just feels good, drivin' around and seeing all the people I went to high school with, the ones that doubted me. They see my truck, and they're like, "Oh boy, he's doing good for himself." I have to sit back and just smile. It makes you feel good. Especially because it's a truck!

Around these areas, we love our trucks. I mean you have not experienced anything until you hop in a truck and drive through the mountains with no idea where you're goin'.

I can do that with this truck. It's me with my truck, me with the people I'm with, and I'm just cruising. I have not a worry in the world. I'm graspin' nature. It's the best feeling in the world. I don't know why he keeps coming up, but Justin Moore sings another song, "Flyin' Down A Back Road." It by far defines the feeling that I get when I'm driving down a back road.

A vehicle that goes off road, like a Jeep—if it doesn't have a bed, it doesn't make sense. What happens if I need to help someone move? What happens if I want to take a girl for ride and we get up and we wanta star-gaze if I don't have a bed to lay in? A truck is everything you want.

So far I've changed the headlights, revamped the interior, and put in the Mossy Oak floor mats, windshield visor, and the sunscreen, and I got stickers. All trucks need to have stickers. And every piece of chrome you see on that truck will disappear. I do not like chrome. To me, it's a different generation. Back in the day, they loved chrome. So many people overuse chrome. Those rims on that truck, they're gonna be black. With a white truck, black and white looks amazing!

When someone has a truck, they have to make it look good. I don't know how much I can stress that. That is my incentive. Okay, this may sound weird, or

wrong—but I'm only 19 years old. That truck out there is my kid, and I'm gonna do everything to make it the biggest and best, the strongest kid on the playground.

It also has to sound good, it does. When you're driving down the road, people are going to look at your truck. This happens to me all the time and makes me feel good. "Ah, I love your truck. That's one badass Chevrolet." I love it. They're saying stuff when they see it, and I want them to continue saying stuff when I'm driving away. It makes me feel good that the people who have put me down in the past are sitting there talking about me.

DAVID HILTY

*It's a personal relationship.
Trucks are very friendly to drive.*

When we retired out here, my son said, "Gee, Dad, what are you going to do with all that land? Maybe you ought to consider growing some grapes." My wife and I took courses and thought we'd try. After a while, I said, "I think I'm gonna start making some wine." My wife said, "No, you're not—you don't know anything about it." But I did, and it got better and better. It's a very good avocation for somebody my age who wants to be outside all the time.

I deliver wine with my truck, and I'm constantly hauling pieces of my tractor for repair or hauling brush or picking up bad fruit to haul to the trash pile. But the truck is not a business truck—it's for personal use. I'd have to say it's a personal relationship. Trucks are very friendly to drive. There's a lot of flexibility, and it's a means of relaxation.

GEORGE FIELD

I love history.

I got interested in having a pickup because it would be the easiest thing to repair and restore. Of course I found out later they were all prone to rust real bad. As the saying went, they rusted when they were leaving the factory. But it turned out that there are a lot of relatively simple fixes for the usual rust-out spots. People made what they call patch panels. It turned out to be quite an industry, which perseveres today.

This is a '56 GMC. It is an unusual one in that it has what they called a Deluxe Cab and other accessories. It came from the factory with two-tone paint. The whole front end of the thing was chrome plated—the

bumper and the grill work. You could order it that way. I don't think many dealers stocked 'em like that. How it got to be back in the country, sittin' in this old warehouse, I don't know.

This thing had something called road shock dampers. I didn't know what they were. Nobody else did either! I saw in one of the vintage ads that I had collected that they had a reference to the thing. And I said,

"Lo and behold, there they are." And I had 'em. It had the original radio in it, too.

Whoever had it last put in this old 4-speed transmission and cut a hole in the floor for the gearshift. That steering column had been replaced from probably a '57. So we had to find a steering column somewhere. I did the interior myself. I was much younger then. I could waddle around in there on my haunches, spraying and carryin' on. I got the bed at a junk yard. It turned out to be a three-quarter ton, which was an even longer bed, and so it cost me.

When I bought the bed, the fenders came with it, and the fellow told me I needed a dimple for the fender. These fenders have a dimple in 'em to make room for the spare tire. He had a fender with that in it, and the fender was a total piece of rust except that part was good. He cut it out of that fender and gave it to me and said, "Now you get your body man to put that in one of those fenders."

I finally painted the inside. And these are the right colors. I got some paint codes and color charts and

information about what interior went with what exterior on the Deluxe Cab version. I enjoy the research part, and I love history. It got frustrating at times because there aren't many people who knew much about it. The old-timers are fading, and so lots of valuable sources disappear.

Having the truck finished is more fun than restoring it. Whew! That was an experience I couldn't do again. It was almost a ten-year project.

I used to use it a lot more as a truck. Very carefully, but I used it. Now I drive it for exercise. I occasionally take it in a parade, and if the club is going to some event where somebody wants an old vehicle, we'll go.

Original engine, rebuilt

NANCY SLYE

Running around in a pickup truck in New York—that was not a cool thing to do. But down here? No problem.

I use it as a trash can—it's a great trash can. And I use it to move stuff from the library where I volunteer. We move animals with it, too. Besides peacocks, I raise llamas, Angora goats, sheep, cattle, and chickens. And I have three ducks left—the fox got most of my duckies.

For running a farm, a pickup is indispensable. I can't do without one. But do I love it? Actually, it's very comfortable—probably more comfortable than my car. My first pickup truck was very uncomfortable. I wore that one out. When I bought that pickup truck, everybody sort of looked down their noses at me. I was in Westchester County, New York, and I was a woman, and I was married to an executive. There I was running around in a pickup truck. That was not a cool thing to do! I loved it. I

Beware of Grumpy Dog & Vicious Old Lady

thought it was wonderful. But it wasn't cool—not in Westchester in the '80s. But down here? No problem. Everybody around here drives a pickup truck.

It's always been my desire to be a farmer. My grandfather had a farm on the Chesapeake Bay, and I spent every summer there. I just like farming and all the stuff that goes with getting your nails dirty.

DAVID SAUNIER AND PAUL SAUNIER

> *I feel a little more connected to the earth and to labor and to basic, simple things when I'm in my truck.*

DAVID: We have a 1976 Chevy Cheyenne Special Camper Edition. And it's a great truck because it's designed to haul a lot of weight and do a lot of work. My twin brother, Paul, and I bought it very used. We got it primarily because we share this property up in the mountains, and we used to take cattle up there and do various things.

Earlier I had a truck as my primary vehicle. But after I got married and had kids, it wasn't a practical vehicle. So I got rid of

that truck and just had a car. But then we no longer had a truck to do some farming stuff.

PAUL: One of the many reasons we got the truck is because we used to have cattle up there, and each year we bought two or three head of cattle.

DAVID: It's ironic. Ever since buying this truck we haven't gotten any cows. We still do other farm things, but I use the truck more than my brother.

PAUL: Basically, David has the truck. I don't see it very often.

DAVID: He sees it whenever he wants to. He has visitation rights. We own it together, yet I'm the beneficiary, quite frankly.

I was a carpenter for many years. My truck was my primary vehicle. Now I have this desk job. One of the things I really enjoy about the truck is that when I'm using it, I'm doing physical work. I would feel something was lost if I didn't have the truck. That's what I have it for. It's a work truck, as you can see—not a show truck.

I feel a little more connected to the earth and to labor and to basic, simple things when I'm in my truck. And it's a basic, simple truck. The radio doesn't function, the heat doesn't work now, and the AC never worked in our experience. There's this obnoxious white button on the dash that functions as the horn. I have to take both hands off the wheel to hit the horn.

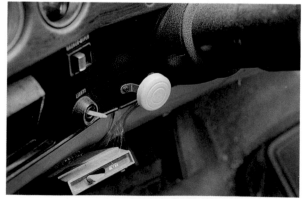

It just has countless small problems that I develop a kind of affection for as things fall apart.

I have three daughters, and one is very excited whenever we have reason to be in the truck. One of the others is embarrassed because we're driving a beat up old truck. I took them to school today. One was embarrassed, and one was excited. The embarrassed one wanted us to park and not be in the line of cars. The other one couldn't have been happier.

I think trucks are made for work. I personally find something a little unnatural about a truck that doesn't do work. Things have their purpose. A truck that somebody is worried about getting scratched is just not being a truck. It's not being properly used.

My 5-year-old and 4-year-old girls love to play on the truck. It's funny, because now I remember that my twin brother and I would play on our neighbor's truck when we were very, very small. Often when we could not be located, we were in Mr. Brown's truck. I think at some point my parents found us there as 4-year-olds, naked in the back of Mr. Brown's truck. We felt we no longer needed to wear clothes when we played in Mr. Brown's truck.

People like to borrow trucks. I think there's even a bumper sticker on that theme—something like, "Don't ask. I will not loan you my truck." During that brief period of time when I didn't have a truck, I remember asking a friend of mine if I could borrow his truck, and he said, "No." That struck me as odd, because I'm certainly always willing to lend out my truck.

We had some trouble with the truck because it has two gas tanks. One of the gas tanks was turned off, unbeknownst to me, and there was a miscommunication between us. Basically, I was running out of gas, thinking I was using the right tank, but I wasn't using the correct tank. The shut-off is broken. Paul had it disconnected.

PAUL: No, it's not disconnected.

DAVID: You said it was disconnected.

PAUL: I did not.

DAVID: You told me you had it disconnected because it was leaking.

PAUL: That was fixed. That's been fixed a long time ago.

DAVID: They're both functioning?

PAUL: Yeah.

DAVID: I'm not so sure that's the case.

PAUL: That's your experience, not mine. The one time it leaked, there was a hose that had to be replaced up near the top.

DAVID: I think it has been shut off. I noticed very clearly because I ran out of gas with the little girls just last week.

This truck is a wonderfully useful thing. I really do have an identity thing tied into it related to work. It's not so much a reminder of the past. What I like more is that it roots me in the present. My idea of a great day is not at my desk—it's out in the world doing manual labor. So I hope I always have a truck. It'll be a sad day if I no longer feel the need to have the truck. I'll have moved away from doing the sort of work that I get a lot of pleasure from.

I've always enjoyed a vehicle that was struggling and was just kinda on the edge. It has a sort of romance to it when every drive is an adventure. Our truck has its problems, but that's part of its appeal.

David and Paul

CHARLES BELL

It reflects my personality— always ready to be helpful.

I've had this pickup for ten years. I got it through a friend of mine. I just went looking for a vehicle, and he said, "We have this truck. Take a look at it, drive it home, come back in a couple days." And I fell in love with it. Excuse me, we fell—my wife and I.

I do a lot of gardening, and I wanted to transport the produce. This truck is very, very handy for anything—to take the trash or haul tables and chairs at the church.

I taught Grades 8, 9, and 10 for thirty years. And I was on the Board of Supervisors of the county for twelve years. I've always been active in the community. Now that I'm retired, I do community service. I teach Sunday school on Sunday mornings. I've always been active in the community, trying to assist and support kids and farming.

This truck reflects my personality—always ready to be helpful. I try to be anyway.

JERRY HANSON

Since I'm a Harley-Davidson nut, I wanted an orange truck.

Trucks never interested me until I was about 45. Before that I was a motorcycle nut. You just kind of go through different phases about what you wanta fool around with.

I was on eBay one night, and I saw this '66 Ford pickup truck. It was right outside of Charlotte, North Carolina. I got on my Harley, and I went down there. The following weekend I borrowed my friend's truck and trailer, bought the truck, and brought it home. I worked on the truck for about two years, and then I took it to some shows. I've gotten about six trophies or plaques with it. It's a show

truck more or less. It's just a hobby.

It doesn't have the original motor. It's got a 302 in it. I had to put another head on the motor, and then I put a 4-barrel aluminum intake on the engine with a Holley carburetor. The transmission had a 3-speed in it, and I put the Ford 4-speed in it. And I put a car rear end in it for a higher gear. Now I can cruise at 65 miles an hour with no problem at all. Of course, there ain't no power steering on it.

It was purple when I brought it home. Somebody painted the thing purple! I brought it home, and all the neighbors laughed at it. What's wrong with this guy? What d'ya want that piece of junk for? I tried to keep it covered up, so nobody would complain about it. And when I got done with it, they said, "Jerry, I had no idea it would turn out like that."

Since I'm a Harley-Davidson nut, I wanted an orange truck. But I got to thinking that Harley-Davidson orange just didn't look right on there. That's why I picked out this color—something like an orange and a copper color. When the sunlight hits it, it really catches the eye 'cause it's got the pearl in it. People wanta know what color it is, and I say it's a "Mitsibitchie" car color. That gets a lot of comments. The color really sets it off.

My daughter says this truck is gonna be hers. I used to take her to school in my other truck—it was all spotted up and primed up. I had to drop her off before I got to the school house, so the kids wouldn't see her get out of the truck. But she's 28 years old now, and she's proud of this one.

I did this all myself. It's hard to believe how it turned out in the end. You gotta have a little mechanic and some body-work fundamentals about you before you can do stuff like this. And you just don't do it overnight. It takes time to do this stuff.

MARK GREHLINGER

> ## *I'm more impressed with longevity than I am with power.*

We get a lot of people who come into our lot and look at a truck and say, "Wow, 150,000." To them, it's a huge number. So I just point over to this and say, "There's one with 800,000. It's never been torn down. It's the original motor." And they're like, "Wow." They can't believe it.

When I bought it, I said, "I really wanta know—this was never rebuilt, right?" And he said, "No way. We hardly even changed the oil in it." So it's not taken care of very well. The thing was run as a company truck. Everyone ran it; no one took care of it.

These twelve valves are amazing motors—in my opinion, the best small diesel in the world. That motor was used in Case farm tractors. They use them in small freight haulers and school buses. They're an amazing motor.

It could be all repainted and done up but that kinda takes away from it. It's got the patina on it, as they say. I'm more impressed with longevity than I am with power. Anyone can have power, but there's not many who can say they got that kinda miles. And it's still reliable. I probably could take it to California. I probably wouldn't get there real fast, but I could get there.

TOMMY STARKS

Aw, you got the kitchen sink!

Everybody used to say, "You got everything on that truck except the kitchen sink." I finally put one up there. Now they look up and say, "Aw, you got the kitchen sink!" Well, I got stuff in it, too.

I'm a mason—stone and brick and all. This is my main work truck. Got most of my tools in it. When I'm on jobs, homeowners say, "How in the world do you find things in that truck?" I can find it. They call it a Tommy load.

My other truck has 400,000 miles. See what the tags say? My Toy 87. One of my hens is laying in there—got five eggs in it now. You'd never believe the places that truck's been. But it's still the same motor, the same transmission. All I need to do is put plugs in it.

The Toyota was my favorite truck, but my favorite baby now is the '92 S10. It's a gas saver, and I can take most things I need. If I can't get them in the truck, I hook up a small trailer behind it.

I've been here on this land all my life. This land has been in the family almost a hundred years. I'm here and still here. Ain't many people can say that. There were six of us—all born with a midwife. Never a hospital. See my ridin' pardner, my dog? We're all here.

APRIL DAWE AND TIM DAWE

Quite the adrenaline rush!

TIM: This is a '76 Ford F-250. My daughter, April, and I spent about two years building it. The entire truck, other than the headers, was built at my house in the garage. It's all hand-built by the two of us and our friend, Brian Magaha.

APRIL: We made the truck pulls a family event.

TIM: We just wanted something for the family to do together that was safe—to have a good time and occupy some people's extra time.

APRIL: This is my second season. We

actually got second place last year at the fair. That was pretty exciting. Quite the adrenaline rush! It can be a little scary though when the truck hops real bad. No two tracks are the same, and it's not the same each time on the same track either. Sometimes the track is better at the beginning of the race, so you never know. It's always new.

TIM: It's always a challenge. There's nothing easy about it. But that's what makes it fun.

APRIL: A lot of fun! My boyfriend, Andrew Surface, has the orange truck—the Virginia Redneck. This is how we met—at a truck pull.

TIM: Last year we did something like twenty-three pulls. This summer we have only fifteen or sixteen. It will give us a little break. We have a pool at home that we haven't used very much in the past year or so.

The name of our truck is Endeavor. It was gonna have a different name, but after spending the second year on it and after all the aggravating issues we ran into, we changed its name.

APRIL: Mom said it should have been called Pain in the Butt. This was somewhat of a father/daughter project—this past season especially. The one before that, as the time was getting closer, I was getting fed up with it. I was like, "I don't want to. I'm scared." The very first pull I was absolutely terrified. But it got a lot better.

TIM: She and her mother sat down at a table and went through an entire chip book, and this green was the color they picked. That's a Chevrolet color.

Rear springs are disabled on pulling trucks.

Andrew Surface and April Dawe

APRIL: Trust me—we hear about it!

BYSTANDER: Look! She's got Andrew's orange on!

APRIL: My toenails are both colors. Andrew wouldn't let me paint them just green. I asked him to paint his green. I don't see that happening!

This will be Andrew's and my first full season together. It'll be interesting. He's already told me I'm not winnin' anything. He thinks he's gonna beat me every time. We shall see!

ANDREW SURFACE

I was born in Virginia, and that's how it is.

It's all about winning. None of us show up to come in last. But when you stop having fun, you oughta quit. And there are times when you want to quit. About mid-summer, you start to feel like this truck business is its own little job. You go to work, and then you gotta work on the truck all night.

One time last year, I pulled on a Friday night in Culpeper, and I blew the transmission apart in my truck. I got home

at 1 o'clock at night, and we worked on the truck until 4 or 5 o'clock in the morning. I had to put a new transmission in it to be ready to pull the next day in Warren County.

You have to have at least one extra of everything—or at least know somebody that's friendly enough with you to let you borrow whatever you need. Since I've been pullin', I've blown up six motors—three of 'em were in one season. My buddy, Brad, let me borrow a spare engine to finish the season.

I bought this truck when I was 14. It was in pretty rough shape. Me and my dad restored it, and I drove it the whole time I was in high school. When I went to college, I turned it into a pulling truck. Now it's pretty much a totally different truck. I upgraded the rear end, the front end, the transmission, and the transfer case. It's been through countless motors. Each year I run it, I mess with it as I go. And I get ideas about what I want to do in the down time during the winter.

Probably the most memorable memory I have of the truck was my party—when I graduated from high school. We had a farm, and all my buddies bet me that I wouldn't try to drive the truck across the five-acre pond. So I did it. I made it three-quarters of the way across. When I stopped, water was halfway up the windows. The engine seemed to be all right at the time, but it didn't take too much longer for it to need to be worked on. That water wasn't very good for it.

That name—Virginia Redneck—has been on my license plate since I put the truck on the road. All through school, I was considered a red neck. I was born in Virginia, and that's how it is.

My dad's been pulling since 1995, and now he's the tech official for this class. And my mom is class rep for this class. So for me, it's a family thing. When we go to a pull, it's the family. But that's how it is with most everybody. Girlfriends, boyfriends, mothers, dads, uncles—everybody comes.

NOTE: *On the evening of this interview, the track was a mess because of misuse and rain. Andrew came in third, and April was twelfth. Both earned a purse and were happy with the pull. At the end of the season, April finished fifth in points, and Andrew was sixth.*

APRIL: Andrew's truck broke at the last pull, which is how I got in front of him. Poor guy was not very happy about it.

Our class is the 6,200 mod street. When we pull up on the tracks, our trucks cannot weigh over 6,200 pounds. You try to take as much weight off the back of the truck as you can. To compensate for that, you put it all up in front. The sled will hold your rear down, but you need something to keep your front from wanting to pull up. You gotta be one with your vehicle. You gotta know how it feels. If you give it too much gas too soon, it's gonna spin out. If you don't give it enough gas soon enough, it won't be able to pull out.

APRIL: Some of these trucks have a whole lot of money in them. It's a little advantage, but not necessarily.

ANDREW: Depends where they spent the money. If they spent it in the motor and got a good drive train, it does give an advantage. But the ones that are just pretty—pretty's not a very good advantage.

APRIL: My green is better than any old orange.

ANDREW: I wouldn't say that!

HARVEY YODER

It's more of a Charlie Brown kind of thing.

This is a '97 Nissan pickup. One of our good friends wanted to sell it, so he let us have it for a very reasonable price. He had taken care of it so well, and of course I try to do the same.

I don't know how I would do without a pickup. It is so handy, so practical, and useful.

We just have a half-acre lot, but we burn wood. I have my own chain saw and cut our own wood. It's good exercise, and I enjoy it a lot. And I like to garden. So when I need to haul mulch, some horse manure from my neighbor, or something like

that, it is just so nice to have a pickup. And I use it to go back and forth from work.

It fits in with my pragmatic nature. I'm big on getting exercise. I'd much rather do exercise that's useful, and the same way with this. It's fun to have the pickup, but you get to do a lot of useful things with it. Plus I enjoy loaning it to my friends. There were years when I had to borrow a pickup every now and then for something. So I just enjoy being on the other side of that and letting other people use it.

These days, people—men especially—like these huge, massive V8s that make this truck look like a pygmy. So it's not a prestige vehicle, for sure. I love it anyway. It's certainly not like the mid-life sports car that's going to make me look bigger, younger, whatever. It's more of a Charlie Brown kind of thing.

BILL GOLDBERG

> *It's one of the last links to my long hair, Grateful Dead, hippie days.*

My truck is a 1985 Toyota pickup that I've owned since 1995. It had about 70,000 miles on it when I got it, and now it has about 175,000. I was moving to Texas, and I was somewhat homeless at the time. I was looking for something that I could put my stuff in as well as sleep in occasionally.

A lot of our drives to and from Texas had their comical parts. Picture this: two or three long-haired guys who've just finished movie work. Our typical dress in winter was cut-off shorts with thermals underneath and flannel shirts. Yes, it's what you picture. Austin is a very safe area—

I think someone called it the liberal middle finger in the state of Texas. But driving to the border of Texas and through Arkansas was always a little touchy. You wanted to be on your best behavior for the drive.

Once we stopped in Arkansas for dinner, and it was just like a scene out of *Easy Rider*. The three of us walked into the restaurant, and all conversation stopped. It was just dead silence, people staring at us. Neither of my friends had seen *Easy Rider*. I told them about that scene, about what happened to Jack Nicholson after that scene, where he

was killed. We ate dinner very quietly and then left. We decided we were not stopping anywhere that night. We were just going to drive through.

There was also the time on the road when I woke up in the back of my truck surrounded by three semis that were eight to ten inches from each of my bumpers. My idiot friend who was driving had cut off one of them and apparently that one had called his friends. They surrounded us, and there was nothing we could do for ten to fifteen miles; that's the way we drove.

I mean—it was great. I have a cap for the truck, so we would just take turns. One person would drive, and the other would sleep in the back. We did that up until I moved up here. After our daughter was born and my wife, Lisa, was making trips to D.C., we ended up buying a second car. We didn't really want to get rid of the pickup. It had a lot of value and a lot of sentimental value for me. But we also realized that having three cars for two drivers probably wasn't the best in a "live simply" community.

So our idea became to leave it up here at the university and make it open for anybody in the community who needed a truck. It's probably been used by at least eighty or ninety people. Most people are polite enough, and they call. But sometimes I've shown up at the office, and my truck hasn't been there, and I've had no clue where it was.

I've always believed that not everybody needs everything. It doesn't make sense for everyone to have a

truck or to have to rent one to move a sofa. So this is what I can give to the community. It's worked great.

In the past couple of years, I've realized that several of our graduate students are actually younger than the truck. That was an odd turning point when I started

telling people, "It's available, but be careful with it because it's older than you are."

This past summer the truck needed new tires. A faculty member took up a collection and raised about two-thirds of the money for the tires. That was great. I had to get it inspected this fall, and it didn't pass inspection. So this might be the end of my ownership of it.

It's kinda sad. It's one of the last links to my long hair, Grateful Dead, hippie days, traveling around the country and sleeping in the truck before I got responsibility—a job and a family. It's the last part of my past, and it's a bit difficult to let go. I love being married, I love having two children, but there is a certain wild streak in me that's been slowly ebbing out. This is one of the last vestiges of it.

GERALD YOUNG

I'm just in a world of my own, enjoying myself.

If I buy another truck, my wife will divorce me! I had a black truck that I did from scratch, from the ground up. I decided to sell it—like a big dummy. I sold it, and then I kicked myself. I sat on the steps for two weeks crying. My wife said, "You must love me.

You sold the truck." I said, "If I didn't love you, you'd be gone, and the truck would still be here."

This one I got about ten years ago. I decided I wanted a hot rod truck to enjoy myself—to think I'm a teenager again. That's what it's about. It's trying to go back to our childhoods, back to our teenage years. And it's goin' out talkin' to people, enjoying the life. I'm just in a world of my own, enjoying myself.

I'm a diabetic. My blood sugar was a problem, and when I got in this truck, it went away.

I like Ford—always Ford. This truck's got a small block 302 Mustang motor out of an '85 Mustang. It goes down the road! I had it up to 110 one time. That was one time. The rest of the time, it's going between 45 and 50. I'm too old to get a ticket now.

BETSY MAPP

It's like an extended pocketbook.

I bought it brand new, right when all of the automotive companies were in terrible financial condition. I have faith in Chevrolet products and felt that they would come back from the brink. And sure enough, they are. I was brought home from the hospital when I was born in a 1938 Chevrolet, and I was in Chevy's for my whole childhood.

I live on a farm, and I'm constantly having to haul brush or firewood or bags of stuff. I usually have rakes and shovels and post-hole diggers and all kinds of stuff back there. It's like an extended pocketbook because behind the scenes, I've got all kinds of stuff.

I use my pickup locally, runnin' back and forth from my house to other local areas. It means everything to me—good on gas, not too flashy looking. It's part of my identity because I support farmers, and they're under siege these days with ruinous tax rates. I think being an outspoken advocate for farming might help turn the corner politically.

~ *Pickups: A Love Story*

"DOC" ART CARTER

> *What better vacation than for a man to have his hunting dog, his shotgun, his pickup truck, and his wife all together?*

In 1983, I bought my first Dodge pickup truck when I moved from the city to the country. My Mercedes was not appropriate, in my opinion, for the life I wanted to live out in this rural area of Virginia. I had sold my medical practice in Norfolk and opened my practice here on the Eastern Shore.

My interest in hunting started as a child, and my father taught me. He was taught the pleasure of bird hunting by older men in this community—especially the pleasure of hunting with a well-trained dog. Coming back here, I wanted to get back to those roots.

I go out with my pickup truck and dog and walk around for hours. Part of the fun is just being out walking around. It's so peaceful. I don't care whether I get anything or not. The real pleasure is walk-ing behind a well-trained dog and the beauty of that pointer or setter working the hedgerows and the tree lines.

I had my Dodge pickup truck and decided that instead of the vacations my wife and I had been going on with our children, I would suggest to her that we might do something different. I said to her, "Honey, I'd really like to drive out to the Dakotas and camp out on the prairie with my bird dog, Ty. I'd hunt, and we could eat off what I am able to harvest during the day, and I'd like you to go with me."

She reminds me that the first thought in her mind was, "Oh my! The man lost his mind!" And then she thought, "Here he is in a medical practice, and God knows I've seen so little of him, day and night. Here's a chance to spend some time with just the two of us. So I'll go." That's what started the journey.

I had my gun rack, a shotgun on the rack, and my dog and wife in the front seat next to me. We had some local Eastern Shore wine and a bag of frozen local Eastern Shore strawberries. We headed down the road to drive across country and to spend some very precious time in the Dakotas. Around here when I hunt, the dog sits in front with me. So my wife and I started out down the road with the dog in the front seat between us. The dog was so happy, he was slobbering over my wife. We got a mile down the road, and my wife had to stop at her office to drop something off. By the time she came back from the office, the dog was in the doghouse in the back.

We camped on the Missouri River in a state park. I put an Oriental rug on the floor of our tent, an air mattress on the Oriental rug, and sleeping bags on the air mattress. I brought a DVD player and put in Miles Davis, opened the local Eastern Shore wine, and brought out the

strawberries. That was our first night in the Dakotas.

My wife would read, and I'd go out and hunt. And whatever I hunted, I'd bring back and clean and roast, and we'd eat it together. What better vacation than for a man to have his hunting dog, his shotgun, his pickup truck, and his wife all together? Vacations don't get any better than that!

So that was my Dodge pickup truck. The next truck was a Ford 4-wheel drive. I've had this Chevrolet Silverado 4-wheel drive since 2003. All three of these—Dodge, Ford, Chevy Silverado—are trucks that we locals say are for different types of people. We say that the Dodge Ram is typically a young man's truck. He's going be taking it everywhere—just rolling through the woods— doing all kinds of hunting and fishing and things. The Ford pickup truck, we say, is for the person who's going to use it for work, for transportation, and for hauling. And we typically say the Chevrolet— because it is much more comfortable—is for old men. And that's where I am with my life.

Now we are a one-vehicle family. My wife's car died last year, and we decided that rather than buy another car, we would see how it would work to spend more time together. We talk about how surprised we are at how well this is going. We've negotiated that the right side of the truck is hers, because she has unintentionally branded it a few times. "That's okay, Baby, we'll just let your side be branded all you want," you know. With that half, she can do what she wants.

Peter Jacob Carter is one of my ancestors. He represented this rural county, and historians say he was one of the longest-serving African-American members of the Virginia House of Delegates during the Reconstruction years. A pickup truck back then would have been a team of horses or mules and a wagon with a seat on the front—like a pickup truck and a flat bed on the back. Those were the pickup trucks of their day. Horsepower was really horses.

I don't have a name for the truck. I do refer to her as a she, though. She's gentle, she's reliable, and she's strong. She's a she. The older she gets, the more comfortable she gets.

TOM HAYMAN

This is my mobile coffee shop.

This is my mobile coffee shop. It's where I do the brewing and the grinding, and it's my means of conveying everything we need to the market. I enjoy really good coffee with people. When I'm roasting I'm by myself, so I'm very much in my own world, and this gives me a place where I can meet people.

The truck is a 2008 Nissan Frontier with a crew cab. It's only a four-foot bed, so it's kinda crowded. But it's got four seats, which is good since we have two children. My wife would prefer that we have a minivan, but I draw the line at that.

This setup is working pretty well. I think if we were making more money, it would be easier to sell my wife on the idea of fixing the truck up more, but we're not. If it ain't broke, don't fix it.

LOIS BOWMAN

> *It's not what I'd call pretty,*
> *but it sure is comfortable.*

My husband, Wade, built the camper. A friend told Wade he had this pickup bed, and he could make him a trailer. I had told Wade that one thing I didn't like about commercial campers was that everything was locked in place, and you didn't have any flexibility.

So Wade made the camper to fit the trailer. Wade grew up on a farm, and they learned to do everything they needed to do for themselves, so

he just thought this up. He didn't have a pattern to go by.

He started it, then got discouraged, and just stored it way. One evening when our daughter, Wanda, was in Bible school, we said, "Let's go look at campers." When we started seeing price tags, we came back, and he pulled this out of storage and kept on with it. I lent a hand as I could.

Our first camping trip with it was June 1974. The old Pontiac that we used to pull it had such a sad face that we called it Eeyore. The camper on the trailer, bouncing along behind, became Tigger. We bought the truck in '95 and got the camper on in time to go camping that summer. I'd have preferred any color but brown, but I've gotten used to it.

When Wade made it, he had to make the top in three strips across. He sealed it well, but once we were up at Loft Mountain, and the weather was very, very hot. Then a cold thunderstorm came along, and it just cracked all those seams. After that, I don't know how many times I saw Wade climb up on that roof and reseal those seams. It never held, so one year when he was on dialysis, I got in there and loosened all the bolts on the roof. A niece and her husband helped me lift it off. I took that roof apart, put in new insulation, and replaced the wooden strips.

It's not what I'd call pretty, but it sure is comfortable. Since Wade's gone—he's been gone for eleven years—my sister, Ruth, and I go camping together. I don't use it a lot, but Ruth and I try to take it out every month or so just for a little jaunt in the country. It's interesting when we're camping. People stroll around the campground, and sometimes men will stop and ask questions about it. They want to know how it was made and all that.

MIKE: Mine is an '82 Chevrolet short bed truck. My neighbor and I restored it and put a V8 in it. I lowered it three inches in the front and five inches in the back. It's seldom I go down the road and stop someplace and somebody doesn't make a comment about it or wave or something. It's a good feeling. Once in a while we'll take it up to D.C., and we'll come to a traffic light. All the office girls at the crosswalks getting ready to cross are just amazed at the truck. They're oohin' and ahhin', just lookin' at the truck. It's kinda funny—you never imagine a lady would be lookin' at a truck.

JOHN: Mine is a '57 Chevy pickup, a short bed. When I was a kid, the first car I owned was a '57 Chevy. I just like '57s, but I like trucks better than I like cars. It's not as fast as I'd like for it to be, but it's not made to be fast—just for cruising. When it gets hot, I don't go far. The air conditioning is 55 miles an hour, two windows down.

WIL RESSLER

> ## *It is an enjoyable contrast to getting in a big airplane and flying 500 miles an hour.*

My dad bought the truck in York, Pennsylvania. It is a 1990 Chevrolet S-10. He was a salesman and a preacher. He had a little boom box—I guess you'd call it—and tapes from Moody Bible Institute. So he had his little boom box and his tapes, and he'd be driving around and listening to Moody Bible Institute sermons.

My sister and her husband got it in 1998. He was a doctor on a Native American reservation in South Dakota, so it went up there. Then they went to Arizona for work. Then I got it. I picked it up and drove it to Berkeley,

California, where my wife and I were living. Then last year, when we moved back here, I put it on a trailer. I decided it was too old to drive 3,000 miles. It may have made it, though.

A fun part of the story is that my neighbor had given me a bright yellow two-person kayak. My sister was moving to Alaska. They didn't want to take the truck, but they thought they could use a kayak. So I traded the kayak for the truck. And the thing is, somehow I finally ended up with both the kayak and the truck, although they still have the oars.

It's just a great little truck. It's so simple. It's not hard to maintain, although a couple of months ago it was running badly and just coughing really badly. It was losing power terribly, and I took it downtown. They checked out some electronic module and put a new one in. It didn't help much. So I took out the plugs, and the whole inside of a spark plug was missing! It was basically operating on three spark plugs.

When my dad got the truck, it was just as basic as could be: no radio, no air conditioning, no power windows, no power steering. He was a simple man and didn't have a lot of money, and he just bought the very basics. It has a radio in it now—I'm not that simple.

The inside of the back is brown, the original color. My brother-in-law named it Skippy. I don't know if that was after the peanut butter,

Skippy (the pickup) and the kayak in a family quilt honoring family memories

Regarding the quilt, my sister, Willie—who I got the truck from in exchange for the kayak—is very gracious, kind, and thoughtful. Since my parents are gone, she has been the main sibling that keeps the family close, planning events, remembering significant dates, etc. To show our appreciation, family members made patches that my wife and I then put into a quilt that showed a special connection, memory, or thought of her. The one my wife and I did was of Skippy and the kayak.

because that's kind of the color it was, but that's its official name.

In Berkeley we lived in a nice area, and there weren't a lot of trucks that looked beat up in Berkeley. And it was a very disgusting brown and looking kinda rusty and all. It really was becoming a blight in the neighborhood. So I decided I had to paint it. I got twelve cans of blue spray paint and took it up in the woods. Every time a car would come up, I'd duck behind it because I didn't want

people to see. I felt guilty the whole time. You know the environment's very important, and here I am, getting all this spray paint in the air. I didn't get the inside done, but I got everything else done, and actually, except for the glossy finish, it's not a bad job.

I work for United Airlines. I was based in California for twenty-two years, but we just transferred back here a year ago, so now I fly out of Dulles. I've flown nearly everything that United has. Right now I'm flying the 757s and 767s, which are transcontinental—some to Europe and some to Ghana, West Africa.

Part of what makes the truck so attractive, so much fun to have, is that it is so extremely different. With the airplanes, so much of it is computerized even though the pilots do all the takeoffs and landings and handle the emergencies. But part of the attraction of the truck is that it's very simple; it's very slow. It's an extreme contrast to what I do normally. I'm certainly not pushing any buttons in here to make anything happen. There's no autopilot. I'm winding down the windows, shifting—everything's manual. For a while I was driving it back and forth to Dulles, which made it an even more interesting comparison, because I would get out of the airplane and directly into the truck.

My brother and I are now sharing the truck. My son, Alex, may come home for a while, so it may end up with another generation. It's certainly part of the family lore, I guess.

I keep it because there are just so many times that it's useful. It is inexpensive; it's paid off; it doesn't cost much to maintain it. I have some basic mechanical knowledge, so I can maintain it myself. If I sold it, I wouldn't get much for it. It's worth much more keeping it. If it gets ugly, I'll just get more cans of spray paint.

I like to do mechanical work, and I think that's part of the contrast with my job that I like. To be able to come home and work on it—I think it is an enjoyable contrast to getting in a big airplane and flying 500 miles an hour. Get into that truck and drive 55. And that might be pushin' it!

NANCY LINDA JONES

Everybody recognizes this truck.

Everybody recognizes this truck. It's a tough bugger, I tell you. I haul apples sometimes and peaches and things. You can't get much in a car.

I belong to the firehouse. I don't know how many years I've been with the fire company, driving the truck to raffle to raise funds. I picked out the truck every year for 'em. I drove it and sold tickets in it, but I wouldn't know how much money I raised. I broke the record. They don't know how I done it. I go places, and everybody just knows me.

Last day of March I turned 87 years old. I was hopin' I'd be able to help 'em this year, but doctor says I have no business out there. And I know these people miss me now. I worked hard, and I don't regret it. I'm glad I could do it.

WENDI SIRAT

Every day when I drive her, I'm like, "You're the greatest truck!"

I'm a landscaper, and the back of my truck is basically my tool shed. I also play ukulele in the band Mandalélé. All three of us can fit in there with the whole load of instruments and sound equipment. And I have canoe racks so I can put my boat on top. I just use it for everything.

My truck is a 2003 Tacoma that I bought new. It was the first time I ever bought a new truck. I was in a little bit of a desperate situation. I had a lemon, and it was just nickel and diming me left and right. It was a pain, and I needed something reliable. I said, "That's it. I'm goin' to the dealer. He's gonna sell me a truck. I'm gonna drive home with a truck." So I did, and that's my new truck, which I love. I was a little unsure of it at first. I was like, "Oh my gosh, what am I doing? Pay-

ments for five years! Am I crazy?" But I've never regretted it.

It's been awesome. I have 210,000 miles on it now. It's been around the country. We went paddling down the Rio Grande one winter. That was our first big road trip with that truck. I figured, "I've got a brand new truck. I could pretty much drive anywhere there's a road. It doesn't matter how far it is. Where do I wanta go?" I said, "Let's go canoeing down the Rio Grande." So we did. We drove out to Texas—four of us. We spent twelve days, did 116 miles down the Rio Grande, and drove back. It's wonderful. I love it.

I don't have a name for her, but it is a her. She serves me well. Every day when I drive her, I'm like, "You're the greatest truck!"

ROBERT FULK

I love the outdoors, and that's what I use this truck for.

My truck's a '95 Nissan pickup, 3.0, V6. It was the first vehicle I ever had. I got it when I was 15 years old. I mainly just take it hunting and out in bad weather, so I don't have to worry about dinging my other one. It's nothin' pretty.

I mainly coon hunt with dogs. I used to bear hunt a good bit, but I don't have the time for it as much as I used to. I got out of that once I joined the fire department. With coon hunting, most of the time you get to bring your dogs back the same day. Bear huntin' is a more drawn out process because they might run from here to who knows where. Raccoons won't go as far. The license plate stands for Bluetick—that's the kind of dogs that I use. They love riding back there. They saw me putting this dog box on here the other day, and they were getting all excited.

I love the outdoors, and that's what I use this truck for. I'm just a truck guy. I like having 4-wheel drive all the time. I like to have something there if you gotta haul somethin'. And with the fire department, I never know where I'm gonna go. I might go into the mountains or anywhere.

MARSHALL YODER

Unfortunately, it looks like a lawyer's truck.

When I was looking for a truck, I was looking for one that was a beater. I wanted something I could drive around in the woods with the boys—get it muddy and all scratched.

Then I got intrigued by the Mitsubishi Raider because it was the brand that nobody wanted to buy. It had been rejected, and I felt sorry for it. It's not a great truck, not a bad truck. I could have taken a Ford F-150, but everybody's got an F-150. And I thought the juxtaposition of a Japanese name and this southern Raider image was sorta funny. I got a really good deal on it because nobody wanted these things.

It's the most luxurious vehicle I've ever had in terms of the options. The really bizarre thing about the Bluetooth phone system is that apparently it was a company truck, and the voices of the people who used to

drive it are still on this system. So there are names like Bubba's iPhone and Jimbo's, and then one of the guys has Girlfriend. I've always wondered, who's this Girlfriend? It's all voice activated, and it's like the ghosts of the former owners are in this truck.

It is very practical. I use it a lot to haul stuff, and I ride around a lot up in the woods with it 'cause it's got 4-wheel drive, but it's also all-wheel drive. I like it because it can be a family car. I actually can get everybody and the dog in there comfortably. My wife says I can make up all kinds of justifications for getting this truck. But I'm really surprised that I was in my fifties before I got one.

Unfortunately, I would say it looks like a lawyer's truck. It wasn't intended that way, but it was such a good deal.

MATTHEW "GOOSEY" DOLEMAR

Without the truck, I'd probably be just mean!

I've been a Chevrolet man all my life, and I don't like no Fords! All my relatives had Fords, and they stayed in the shop. So I'm a Chevrolet man. My uncle had a truck, an ole '54 Chevrolet, and ever since then I bought trucks. When I bought my first truck, I fell in love with it, and I been having a truck ever since—since I was 18 years old. Don't want nothin' else but a truck. I got a couple cars, too, but a truck is my real thing. I drive it more than I drive that Cadillac.

When I first bought my truck, I lived in a neighborhood where they didn't have trash pickup. People knew I had a pickup, and I'd go to the dump every Saturday. "Goosey, you goin' to the dump this week?" "Yes, ma'am." "Well, I got some trash for you to take when you go." That was my hustle—haul everybody's trash. Yeah, you gotta have a pickup.

That right there is a '93 with 65,000 miles on it. There ain't no rust spots on it nowhere. I keep my vehicles in pretty good shape. And there ain't too many I let drive my pickup. My wife takes it when she wants it, though—I gotta let her take it. But if somebody needs to haul something, I will go haul it for them. I love it. Without the truck, I'd probably be just mean!

Let's put it this way: My pickups are very important to me. If I ain't got a pickup, a Chevrolet, I'm a different person. Everybody that knows me knows I got a pickup. If they want somethin' done, "Call Goosey."

JOHN MURCH

He's always making fun of my little truck.

There's one guy at the lumberyard, he's always making fun of my little truck. Everyone has a big old thing, and I've got this Chevy S-10 and my little trailer, which carries most of what I need. It serves the purpose I need it to serve. One time I hauled a thirty-four-foot gutter across town during rush hour with it!

For many years I've deceived myself that it has better fuel economy. But it probably ends up using just as much gas as a V8, which wouldn't have to work as hard.

The back corner there—you can see the big dent in it. I was working on a house, working fourteen hours a day, week after week after week. I left to go home one night, and I looked up and noticed I had left the skylight open. So I backed up, and it kinda had a resistance. I didn't see anything behind me, but I real-

ized when I got home, "Oh, I got a trailer on there!" It jack-knifed around this side. I was working too much.

People get in there and try to get it started. My wife, Jennifer, often struggles to get it started. I just walk over and kinda jiggle the key a little bit, and it starts right up. It just takes a little touch.

DAVID AND MICHELE VAN PELT

When he starts talkin' about gettin' rid of the truck, I'm gonna get nervous.

MICHELE: When we'd gotten engaged, his mom took me aside and said, "I hope you're not marrying him for his money because dairy farmers don't make a lot of money." I looked at her, and I said, "No, ma'am. I'm marrying him for his pickup truck."

DAVID: We dated a lot in that truck. That was my primary vehicle.

MICHELE: The first time I drove it, we had gone out, and he was taking me back home. I still lived with my parents then. He was in the rescue squad and got called out. He threw me the keys to the truck and said, "Take it over to your mom and dad's,

and I'll pick it up." Well, it was pitch black dark, and I couldn't get it outta grandma gear. I crept my way to Mom and Dad's, and I pulled in the drive, and my dad was waiting up. And Dad looked at me, and he said, "Oh my." I said, "What?" He said, "The boy must be in love. He let you drive his precious pickup truck! That's the only reason a man would let a female drive his truck."

DAVID: She likes to help me work on it. One time I had the front hubs tore apart and was repacking the bearings. She came out and sat down with her long fingernails and popped the grease in her hands and started packing the bearings. A neighbor saw her doing that and—I tell you what—she was hated by all the women in the community for a while 'cause all the husbands said, "Well, why don't you do that?"

MICHELE: I got dirty looks, oh yeah. Somebody asked on our one year anniversary—I had just found out I was pregnant—"Oh, what did you do for your first anniversary?" I said, "Oh, we changed shocks on the pickup truck." "What?" "Yeah, we changed shocks on the pickup truck." "And you did it?" "Yeah. No problem." And that's not the original tailgate. I bought that tailgate for him for an anniversary present.

I had a Volkswagen when I was in high school, and I used to babysit for this couple. He had a garage. Money was tight for them, and the deal was that I would babysit, and he would teach me how to work on vehicles. To me that was a much better deal because

the money would have been long gone, but the knowledge is still there.

DAVID: It's a 1978 Ford F-150 4x4. It's got a 400 engine in it, and it's a 4-speed. I bought it new. It's got the Ranger package and the Explorer package both. That made for a pretty truck. We drove it up until October a year ago, and I wanta restore the thing. I drove it a little bit this morning. Man, I felt just like this is where I need to be—not the truck I've got sittin' out there right now.

MICHELE: He comes walkin' in the house, and I said, "Well, did it feel weird?" and he says, "No. It felt like goin' home."

DAVID: It hasn't led an easy life. I used it around the farm and out in the fields and hauling feed and everything else, and then it's been through two teenage drivers.

MICHELE: The dents on the passenger side—I was over at my mom's, and she's got a chain link fence, and I had to back it up through the gate. My brother—he was gonna direct me—he's saying, "Turn the steering wheel this way." And I'm going, "No, no, I don't want to!" And he's going, "Trust me." And so I turned the steering wheel the way he said. Crunnccch! We'd only been married about eighteen months. I mean, I just knew David was gonna ring my neck. And I was so upset. He didn't say anything, and I said, "Well, say something!" And he looked at me and said, "Well, it's on your side of the truck. You'll have to look at it." I said, "That is all?

You're not gonna yell at me?" I had fully braced myself for being yelled at for denting his truck.

DAVID: I like trucks, but I bought it to use it. So it's bound to get dings and stuff. The front bumper and fender got damaged when it wasn't but about two years old. I took it to have it inspected. I didn't set the parking brake—I just put it in gear and turned it off. The guy reached in and turned the key, and she took off on him. It hit the counter before he could get the key turned off, and it pushed the fender back a little bit and pushed the bumper back. Most people didn't really notice it unless they were really lookin'. It wasn't beat to pieces.

For as long as I've had it, it's gotta lot of stories to it. The old truck's been good. It'll be thirty-four years soon. I can't see getting rid of it. It's old and halfway worn out, but it's just been so much a part of my life.

MICHELE: He's had the truck longer than I've been with him. So when he starts talkin' about gettin' rid of the truck, I'm gonna get nervous.

BOB BAGEANT

I like to go to shows and share the interest with others.

The Diamond T was advertised as the Cadillac of trucks. It was the first truck to come out with a 100,000 mile guarantee. This one is a '48.

It took me about ten years to get it fixed up and restored. They didn't make that many trucks, and they didn't save that many new parts, so today it's difficult to find parts. Sometimes you buy a whole truck to get a few parts and then try to help each other with parts.

Diamond T made trucks for WWI and WWII. They went all around the world because we had wars going on in different parts of the world. After the wars, it was costly to retrieve a lot of that stuff so some of them stayed in a variety of places. There are many of them still there.

It says on the truck, "Don't go more than 60," but 45 is comfortable; at 55 it sounds like it's wound up quite a bit. So I don't like to drive it too far. I use it to go to shows or parades.

The most common question is, "Who made it?" And I say, "Diamond T was its own company." Then I have to explain it's named after Mr. Tilt. That's the T. And the Diamond part was from his father. His father made a very high quality shoe and sold it throughout Chicago. He used a diamond with a T in the middle of it for the shoes. And when the son started making trucks, he wanted quality recognition, so he called it a Diamond T truck. That, I guess, is pretty unique.

Mostly I like to go to shows and share the interest with others. And some of the folks used the trucks—or their parents did—and so you learn more about your own truck and how it was used. These fellows at truck shows lived and

worked these vehicles, most of them, and—if not them, then their parents or grandparents—somebody they knew worked hard with these trucks, and they knew what they were capable of doing.

RONNIE STRAWDERMAN

I feel an honor that I have the knowledge to restore it.

In 1977, I got this Chevrolet, and I've had it ever since. I've redone it, had the transmission rebuilt on it so it can pull trailers. I put a brand new crate motor in it from General Motors. I'm a Chevy man—I've always been Chevrolet.

I started to do all the bodywork. New fenders, new doors. I had a little help from a friend.

It was a work truck. I used it to haul dry wall for my work. Once I had a 33-foot camper, and I crossed the Afton Mountain with it. I pulled her back in second gear and stomped her to the floor. She's on the floorboard, and my father-in-law says, "You're going have to let it off or you're going to blow her up." I said, "Don't worry. It'll be here."

I topped the mountain at 65 miles an hour with that trailer. He couldn't believe that. That truck, we've had a lot of times with it.

Now that the truck is fixed up, it's a show truck. My grandson and I take it to the car shows. I'm going to give it to him when something happens to me. Yes, sir. And all my tools. He told his grandma, "If anything happens to you, I'm gonna come live with you and take care of you." And he will.

I have the window down and people say, "Hey buddy, you got a nice truck." I feel an honor that I was able to do it and have the knowledge to do it.

DOUG MOSS

> *The truck saw all that evolution— from single man to married man to married with children.*

I don't know if you're familiar with Bodatious, the 4-wheel drive mud races here in Virginia. That's the top runner right there, two years in a row in the mud bog. Plus there's a bunch of spots around town where we used to go rootin'—I call it "rootin'"—and there's been several instances where it's come home with nothing but spots to see through on the windshield. My mom would just walk out the door, shake her head, and walk back in. I put Dug It N on my plate for the play on my name and getting dug in a few times. And now my son, Zach, is going to get it, and I'm going to put ZACTUP on the license plate.

Getting stuck stories? Where do you wanta start—at the beach or in the mud? There was this one time when the hubs broke on the front end. We were trying to get out of some of the worst mud, and I got stuck in what we call an artesian well. Water was seeping in through the door hinges.

There was another place I got a little over zealous—the hills I thought I could climb—and it just buried itself down. I opened the door, and basically the land was right there. I could just kinda squat and roll out. We had to walk about a mile to find a pay phone and grab somebody to come pull us out. So it's been hooked up a couple times, but you never admit that when you go 4-wheelin'. You don't tell anybody about getting hooked up. You never got stuck.

It's an '85 model. I graduated from high school in '86, and this was my first car after graduation. Back then 4-wheel drives, especially the mini-trucks, weren't as popular as they are today, so this thing was kinda special back then. I saw it—man, it was love at first sight. You remember that movie *Back To The Future*? The black one they had in that movie—that was like the one I wanted, and this was so close, I had to have it.

So I went home, begged mom and dad, and they co-signed the loan. I was at work one

day, and they actually came to work under the guise they were going to bring me dinner, and they brought the truck. It's got a lot of good memories in it.

My wife and I got married, and this is what we drove. We drove this on our honeymoon to the beach. We had this at the church, and they decorated it. My brother-in-law put sardines on the exhaust manifold. If you look real close, you can see the skeletons. By the time we got a mile and a half up the road, it stunk to high heaven. We didn't lose the smell 'til we hit Virginia Beach. And he put rice in the air vents so when we tried to blow out the smell, stuff was shooting out at us. They also took the muffler off the day before and parked it at the church. When we started it, of course, it was bla*@! It was all noisy. It was cruel.

We drove this to Nags Head once a month. What we liked to do was tie a tow rope to the bumper and drive real close to the water and kneeboard. Naturally the salt water ate it away. The bed—that's the second bed. Down on the main part of the frame, I had to put four support plates—welded 'em on there. And my step-dad—God bless him—he spent hours on his back on a creeper scrubbing the underside here for me. So it does have a couple of band-aids.

It's been through a couple of phases. I've had neon stripes on it, and then no stripes. I did change the bumpers, and of course those aren't factory rims. But it's more preservation than anything—keep it legal, keep it movin'.

Eventually my interest just went away. I don't know if I got old or if the hobby got old or what, but I think a

little of both. I know I definitely got old. I don't think I'd do a few things I used to do. And now I wouldn't even know where to go. Zach probably knows a couple places to go, but I wouldn't know anymore.

ZACH: I'll probably do the same things he did.

DOUG: No you won't either! Ha. My daughter is 21, and this used to be our main mode of transportation besides my work truck. I have a couple of pictures of her in her curly hair sitting over on the passenger side. She was bopping up the road with the curls bouncing. That's always a good memory.

I guess the truck saw all that evolution—from single man to married man to married with children. It's seen it all. Now it's for the next generation. Maybe Zach will be able to drive some kids in it, his own kids.

The truck has caught people's eyes. I've had offers but nothing I've really entertained. When you put a little bit of work into it, it means what it means to you. I think if I ever did seriously think about selling it, my mom would probably beat me.

CONNIE AND JEFF MITCHELL

> *The world would be a better place if everybody had a hot rod.*

CONNIE: Our deal is kind of a family affair. My dad, Buddy, built his truck, a '47 Ford, and has been building 'em since the '70s. He's 84 now, and he's still building hot rods. He helped my brother, Bernie, build his, and then I asked him to help me. My husband, Jeff Mitchell, builds hot rods, but he is so busy, I didn't want to bother him, and I wanted to put on my touch. He's got his ideas, and I had ideas, and I wanted to do it my way. So I got the opportunity with a lot of help from Dad. It took us eight

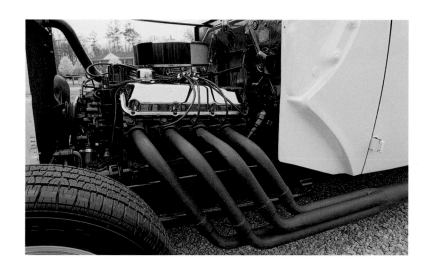

months. We worked on it every day. It was really nice to spend that time with him. It's a family thing. Vehicles have always been a big part of our lives.

It's called a rat rod because it's not one particular vehicle. You just use what you've got. That's the fun part of it—to take and repurpose things. My vehicle actually is mostly the leftover parts from Dad's and Bernie's except for the cab—it's a '46 Ford cab. Half of the grill is a '35, and then Dad and I made the bottom half. We started with a '51 Ford truck chassis

Buddy Napier

and notched it and narrowed it so it fit the '40 Ford front end. Most of it is a '72 Ford pickup—that's what the drive train is. The exhaust system is all handmade and that's a homemade bed. I've even got some lawn mower parts on it. And serious brakes—I'm a mail carrier by trade so stopping is really important to me.

The paint was the darnedest thing. It would not sand. I ended up scraping that entire truck down by hand—with razor blades. It took 500 razor blades! The color shocks people first, and then seeing a woman crawl out of it. They usually are sarcastic when they say, "Well, did you build it?" "Yes, I did!" They kinda step back and look.

I do some interior decorating, and a lot of that goes into it. The motor compartment and interior are black, and the boards in the back are ebony. So I have balance. And my interior headliner I covered with embossed wallpaper that looks like the old ceiling tins. It's just putting a feminine touch on it. But when it

Bernie Napier

came time for the engine, I put the biggest one in it I could find. It's got the 460, and it's been bored out so that makes it a 466. I got a girly truck, but I got the biggest motor!

I think most people really do get a kick out of the fact that it's a family thing. We travel together, and we all help each other. We really enjoy working on them.

A lot of children are drawn to these trucks because they say they look like Hot Wheels trucks. Our grandchildren love riding in them. Our granddaughter said, "You know, Gammy, I think everybody should own a hot rod. Everybody you meet smiles, and you can't help smile when you're ridin' in them. The world would be a better place if everybody had a hot rod."

JEFF: I enjoy driving them, but I probably get more enjoyment out of building 'em. The creative side of it is trying to picture it in your mind and then actually make it come out. You have a lot of artistic freedom when you fool with these. And ninety-nine percent of it is problem-solving. I tell people it's like playing checkers. If you're not thinkin' at least three moves in advance, you've already messed up. Everything you do here is gonna affect something else. So it really challenges your mind to keep you focused and thinking ahead. They're never finished, any of them. You're always going back and doing something.

Like this one. I started out with just the cab—a 1951 Ford cab. I've built the chassis and all that's under that. Even the motor mounts— everything's handmade. I had a picture in my mind of what I wanted the truck to look like. I wanted it to look kinda old school, real low, long in the front, real short in the back, to give it more of a cartoon look.

Most of us are old now, and we're not out there cuttin' up and carryin' on. Law enforcement looks at us and says, "Ah, they're just toolin' down the road and enjoying themselves."

There's a Chick-fil-A here, and every Friday night from April through October there'll be fifty to eighty cars there. We all just congregate out there in the parking lot. It's more of a social event than anything else. It's a chance to get out and talk to friends. And problem solve. I might be doin' something that I can't quite figure out or run into a snag on something. If I talk around to enough people, somebody else has already run into that problem, and they're more than willing to share what it takes to get past that.

We refer to ourselves now as just a bunch of old gray beards. We've raised our families, and now we're getting back to the point in life where we can start to play again. Now we can afford to do some of this stuff.

CHRIS CHAMPEAU

> # I couldn't just go out and buy a Ford F-150 because that's just too boring.

I bought this in Switzerland. It is a Swiss Army surplus vehicle, an ex-troop carrier called the Mercedes Benz Unimog. Most of NATO uses them. This thing is a go-anywhere, unstoppable truck. Four-wheel drive, shift on the fly, locking differentials, and it even has something called portal axles that give it a higher ground clearance capability. These things can go anywhere, climb any mountains.

They were built after WWII as a way for the farmers to get back into farming. It can pull a plow, and it can also take the produce to the market. This one is a '62, but they look almost identical from '55 to '75.

This is a gas, straight-six Mercedes 220 engine—full 84 horsepower, believe it or not. But it can climb; it can rip out stumps. The magic is all in the gearbox. The transmission really makes this vehicle what it is. This thing has six speeds forward and two in reverse, and it has two ranges. Normally, just for everyday driving,

I use third through sixth. The first and second gears are very, very low gears. I normally wouldn't engage those. I use them in reverse, but second in reverse is mostly more than enough.

The seats are not exactly what I'd call real comfy seats. Not only that, but I'm 6′2″ so I have hard time fitting in there. It's challenging. But it's very easy to maintain. It was built for simplicity so that the army guys could easily maintain it on the road. It has push button circuit breakers instead of fuses. If I have an issue, pop that right back, and I'm off and running. The filler for the water is inside so that it can be filled on the fly while it's rolling along.

I couldn't just go out and buy a Ford F-150 because, frankly, that's just too boring. So I had to go over to Switzerland and find this unique vehicle.

BRANDON DERROW

> *You get in behind the wheel of that monster truck and, man, you're gonna have fun.*

The first time I ever went to a monster truck show I was a year and a half old. Every year after that, either Mom or Dad took me. Ever since then I've been crazy about 'em. I fell in love with them, and I always dreamed about gettin' into it.

When we heard this truck was for sale, we got really excited about it. Going through the banks was definitely the roughest part 'cause they didn't want to give us the money on something like that. I must have gone to eight or nine banks, and they just laughed at me, kinda like, "You want money for what?" It all

worked out in the end.

There aren't too many motor sports that are quite as radical. Something that weighs 10,300 pounds jumping thirty and forty feet—it's awesome to see that kind of weight in the air. The suspension and the whole setup—the chassis, the engine—are all special. Going to a show and experiencing it is the biggest part of it, I think. Smelling the smoke, the fumes, man, and seein' 'em in action, that's the best part of it.

The jump is almost every driver's favorite part, what they call the freestyle. You're just kinda out there doing

guys have been in it for a while, and that makes 'em drive that much harder 'cause they don't want to lose to somebody young like me. Some of the guys I've been idolizing my whole life—man, they go all out tryin' to beat us. And money is no problem to some of these guys we're runnin' against, so to beat trucks like Gravedigger and Bigfoot really makes us feel good. We're kind of a low budget race team, and we're competing with these guys. And there's not very many family-oriented monster trucks. I think a lot of people appreciate that.

This year that I've had it has flown by—it was a lot of fun. But I don't think it's quite set in yet that we got the little Hot Wheels truck copies of our truck, Bad News Travels Fast.

whatever you want—the wheelies, the doughnuts, everything. That's really what the fans like. Sometimes they have school buses, motor homes, big obstacles for us to jump.

I'm 24, and I've had the truck just a year. It's been a big learning experience. You not only have to learn how to drive it but to work on it. We're just a family-owned operation, you know. We don't have a lot of extra money to pay crew members. A lot of friends of the family help, too. We do everything ourselves. When we bought this thing, we knew nothing about monster trucks or anything like that. That's the way you learn, I think. Just jump in with both feet and take off with it.

I am one of the younger drivers. Some of the older

I've always liked to have fun, and if you get in behind the wheel of that monster truck, man, you're

gonna have fun. It's always an adventure. And kids love it, man. It always makes me feel good to see all the little kids and the looks on their faces.

Bad News Travels Fast is 11'6" high and 11'9" wide and weighs 10,300 pounds. Its 1700 hp engine runs on alcohol.

ERIC BECK

Business in the front, party in the back.

I had a Tacoma for a long time, and I liked it. I do carpentry work, so I had it set up with my tools. Then last December I quit the company and started my own business so I bought this '04 Ford F-150.

I look at trucks as tools, but also there's personality in trucks. This was kind of a utilitarian purchase. This wasn't my ideal truck, but I felt like I needed a full-size one. We have our farm here, a mini-farm, a hobby farm, and it's nice to have the truck option. So I have a rack, a toolbox, and an open bed so I can throw firewood back there, or I can put racks on the side and put sheep in there. It's kind of cross-utilitarian.

It's a business startup truck. I could get a good deal on it, and it is 4-wheel drive, a V8, and has an extended cab so I could continue

to haul my two girls in there easily. The front end had been pushed in, so I took it down to my brother-in-law's, and we tried to push it out with jacks. Eventually he said, "Clip on to that tree down there." So we chained the bumper to the tree. He said, "Put it in 4-wheel low and start backing up. When I say stop,

you stop." He kept pointing back, and then he got a big grin on his face, and he told me to stop. We were able to pull it out. You can still see it, but it looks fine.

It has a step side in the back. I was a little reticent about the step side because I'm losing some inches, and it doesn't look like a utilitarian construction truck. But I have appreciated it. I call it my aging-in-place truck. I can pull myself up on one of the steps to get to my ladder rack. I started calling it a mullet truck—business in the front, party in the back. It's normal in front, and then you have the little sneaker step side in the back.

SUSAN, ERIC'S WIFE: You've had this relationship with your trucks, but the fact is that you had a hard time having a new relationship with this truck.

ERIC: I haven't really had a bonding experience with this one. I see it more as a tool, a pragmatic tool, than anything else. Yeah, maybe it's a transitional truck, a rebound truck.

PRESTON KELLAM

I'm the pickup man!

I'm the pickup man! I've had a great many of them. I've had very few cars. I got my first pickup when I was 22 or 23 years old. I'll soon be 68.

Right now I have four, but this one is my favorite. I just love driving it. The tires ride real good, but they're twenty inches tall and, believe it or not, it burns more gas with the twenty-inch tires on it. What can I say?

I work a little bit, and I drive a school bus. We're not rich, but we live all right. It'll be a long time until I retire. I love working. I love to depend on myself. Everything I got, I worked for. What can I say? I'm poor, but I love being like that. I'm a survivor. And you can see I have plenty of food to eat! Everybody here, I think they like me. When I'm asked for a favor, I try to do it. We live a good life.

CHRIS FOTTA AND JEANNIE STONE

We're still together; the truck's still runnin'.

CHRIS: This is a '93 Toyota pickup. It came into my life about the same time that Jeannie did. I needed a vehicle, and my friend had this just sitting. It was the best $1,200 that I've ever spent.

That was four and a half years ago, and Jeannie and I have more or less lived in it. It's been the most stable thing in our lives other than our relationship. We worked seasonally and ended up with winters off. We were working in New York State at the time, and Jeannie is from Texas, so we would often make the trip from New York down to Texas as a way to go across country. But the most interesting trip

that we did was going to Alaska. We drove it eighteen days non-stop. It's a little regular-sized cab with a bench seat, so you really get to know and love somebody—or not love somebody.

JEANNIE: When we were semi-dating, at the end of the season, we'd go our separate ways. But then we couldn't stand to be apart, so he was going to drive me home, which was a ten-hour drive, and it was the first time we'd really ever spent any time together. He said, "Well, this will either make our relationship or break it!"

CHRIS: We're still together; the truck's still runnin'.

I often see cars advertised by a second owner. I am the second owner, but the truck looks a lot rougher than that because my buddy had rolled it at one point. You can still see a lot of the scrapes.

JEANNIE: Obviously, it's not aesthetically pleasing to most people. We've been pulled over by border patrols, harassed by cops. At the Canadian border, they took everything out—even checked the panels. Our truck just sent out this vibe of drug dealer, mass arms dealer.

CHRIS: I think that's from Hollywood. I think that people who smuggle drugs look a lot less suspicious than we do.

Part of the way that I connect to it is that I got it through a personal relationship. It's not just off a lot. We didn't buy it new or by research. It was more serendipity that brought it into my life. I needed a vehicle, and I was just having coffee and saying good-bye to my friend for the winter. It happened very organically, which is a big part of how we tend to try to live our lives. It's just with a little bit

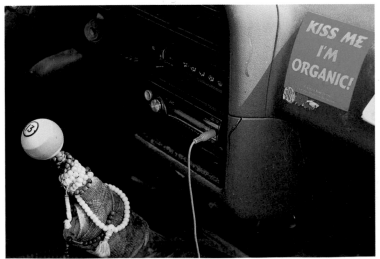

of that faith and trust in the universe providing. So the fact that the truck came when we needed it, and has lasted this long, is symbolic.

We've had multiple mechanics and multiple family members shake their heads about it. My sister's fian-cée is a mechanic, and when I first bought the truck, it had a huge hole in the muffler. He works for a fairly upscale Honda dealership but offered to repair the muffler for me. He got cheers and jeers when he drove it into his bay. At first he was skeptical and shook his head like, "You're going to drive this where?" And

I think now he shakes his head in the other direction, because his much newer, much nicer Subaru has recently blown a head gasket.

People probably don't think much of us with the truck. I think there's that belief that it doesn't look like it would be mechanically sound. We definitely get respect from the other Toyota truck owners, though.

I think it's like the frugality issue—the "can't always judge a book by its cover" issue. It's putting a little bit of trust—putting a LOT of trust—into just thinking and going.

JEANNIE: It's a little bit of a screw-you to the glitzy, TV show style. We don't have to have a brand new car. We don't have a payment; we didn't have

people hounding us when we lost our jobs. And that allows us to do some pretty cool things in our life.

CHRIS: We are farming here, and wherever we settle that's definitely our goal for the rest of our lives—to farm. We hope to give this truck a good retirement some day as a little farm truck. It's also the first pickup truck that I've ever owned. There's definitely something about your first pickup. My hope is that people perceive it as the little engine that could kinda thing. That truck, it'll go.

JEANNIE: Does it symbolize our relationship? It does—until it breaks down.

CHRIS: I think for me it symbolizes more of a specific time in our relationship, and it's a really solid foundation for what we did during that time but also just what's possible. I would say it symbolizes the possibility to do whatever we want, that we have that opportunity to do for ourselves if we want. We hope to have it as a farm vehicle someday. It'll be a reminder of where we started. And even if we cut off the back and make a chicken house out of it, there will be something that we do with part of that truck that will always be with us. So even if it breaks

down, it doesn't symbolize the end of our relationship!

We had to replace the windshield. I was talking to the guy—he hadn't seen the truck yet—and he said, "You can get flat black or get chrome around it." I said, "Black's fine. We don't need chrome." He said, "You might want the chrome; it's only a couple bucks more." "No, when you see the truck, you'll understand." He said, "Alright, let me do this, I'll get both of them in and when you see, you can decide." And as soon as we pulled up, he said, "You need the black." I was like, "Yup." He just wouldn't believe me.

I understand why some people might not love the truck. I love the truck.

⌐ *Pickups: A Love Story*

TOM KAUFMAN

It won't start until I hit the steering wheel.

People say, "What's FAB stand for?" I say, "FABulous." I guess the best way to describe it is that I own a general fabrication shop. As often as I can do race car work, I'll do that. But around here, it's a little hard to find local race car stuff.

I like playing with vehicles—cars, race cars, whatever. And pickup trucks are part of that. They're definitely handy. I like the old stuff. If it breaks down, you can fix it—like this one out here. It's kinda ratty, but if I scratch it, bang it, dent it, whatever, it doesn't matter. I could paint it, but I don't bother. I can put all kinds of stuff back there. It's just tough parking it.

I got it for five hundred bucks. I've had to replace a lot of stuff over the years, but it's still cheaper than payments on a new one. This garbage in the back just appeared in there. When it starts filling up and I need to use it for something, I go to the dump.

It's funny because when I was younger, I always had hot rods, and that definitely was my identity: "You're the guy with the blue Mustang." But once I got into racing, I decided to leave the fast driving to the racetrack and get fewer tickets that way. With that

pickup truck, I don't tend to want to go crazy on the street.

I guess, as much as I hate to admit it, the pickup reflects my personality in that it's kind of a mess, and I'm a mess if you look at my shop. I get really busy. I spend most of my time trying to make ends meet. It doesn't leave a whole lot left over for fixing my things up. Even though I'd like to work on the truck sometime, it's one of those "get around to it" things.

It's just amazing how useful a pickup is. It's almost every single day that I need it for what it is. I can tow my trailer around. I throw stuff in the back here. It's big enough I can sleep in it if I go somewhere and need a bed. And it's a Ford,

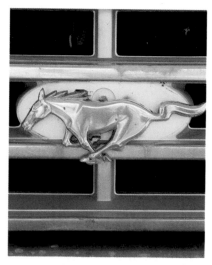

and I'm definitely a Ford guy. I've probably had twenty-some different Mustangs through the years.

The Mustang emblem on front has meaning. That was my identity for many years. I was the Mustang guy. It's a Ford, but I'll work on anything. I'm not one of those guys who is going to put a cartoon on the back window of Calvin pissin' on a Chevy emblem.

I hesitate to let anybody borrow it—not because I'm worried that they'll do anything bad to it, but there are just so many weird things about it. It won't start until I hit the steering wheel. A little tap—I don't have to whack really hard—but that's one of the things. The key doesn't come out. I mean, with great effort I could probably pull it out, but it would be really hard to get it back in, so the key never comes out. I'd have to tell them that: "Don't forget. Don't take the key out."

And then I have to tell 'em, "When you shut it off, turn the radio on. If the radio's on and it's still playing, then you know to put the key in a better position." A lot of times someone will turn it too far, and it runs down the battery.

"And don't touch the fuel tank because it doesn't work right! It'll blow out of the other tank or something. Just don't touch that. The gas gauge doesn't work. You're safe if it's pegged way past full, but if it starts to move at all, you're about to run out of gas." The wipers don't shut off automatically. They'll stop

wherever they are when I turn it off, so I have to time it. It's always a challenge getting them to stop all the way at the bottom.

If I want the dome light to work, I have to push the ceiling just right. It's just all this little stuff. Since I don't take the key out, I always have to leave this side window unlocked. I lock the doors. Not that I really need to lock it, but for some reason I do, and then in the morning I have to punch the window in and reach down and pull up the handle.

When I put it down into drive and take off, I count the shifts because if it doesn't shift, and it feels like it's straining, it's stuck between first and second. So when I put it down into park, I gotta put it down and then bump the shifter up a little bit. I have to make sure that it shifts into third gear. Otherwise it will just be screaming.

There are a lot of weird things like that so I'd rather not lend it to anybody than go through the whole routine and hope they remember everything and don't call me up saying, "Why won't it start?"

It's a great vehicle. I know it, so it's definitely a part of me. Sometimes I'll talk to it, and I'll just say, "Thank you for not stranding me, and thanks for holding together one more day." It has treated me well, I have to say.

A few years ago, we had a financial meltdown like so many other people who invested in real estate. The house was getting foreclosed, and we just decided to take off. Our cousins bought a hundred acres of land in the mountains in Tennessee. They offered for us come out there and just hang out and recuperate, so we took 'em up on it. We gave up most of our worldly possessions in an auction, and what we had left we piled up in the truck. It was quite a pile. It looked like the Beverly Hillbillies, and we were goin' out to the back woods in the mountains, so it was kind of a funny situation. We got a lot of looks and people waving. Yeah. Beverly Hillbillies. We said, "Why don't we put a rocking chair up there?"

In the midst of our disaster we had to sit back and laugh at the whole thing. We were in our fifties, and we were starting over. Here we go! And then we weren't sure the truck would make it. We just had to take it really slow, and it did get us out there. It's actually really been Old Faithful.

Life on the shore is peaceful. There's not a lot of corporate America; there's no traffic. It's just peace and quiet. It's like Andy Griffith's Mayberry. We call it a secret—the land that time forgot—and it's a great secret. A lot of people come here, and they're turned off because there's nothing to do. Well, that's why we're here! It's pretty laid back, and people pretty much leave you alone. The truck fits in with all that.

DAVID SHEPPARD

I'll drive a pickup until I won't be able to drive.

This is a Ford I bought new in '06. I've never done nothing to it but put a bulb in the taillight. It ain't got a whole lot of miles on it. I never drove long distance in it.

I farm, and I cut hair, too. This pickup truck goes seven days a week. I work with it, and come Sunday, I drive it to church. I'd rather have a pickup than have a car. I'll drive a pickup until I won't be able to drive.

JEFFERY WALKER

A pickup — that's a man's vehicle!

I have a 1977 Ford F-100. I call it Midnight. It's my first truck, and I drove it for twenty-two and a half years. I just set it up about two years ago. I said I was gonna sell it, but my children said, "Dad, you know you're not gonna sell that truck. You had it too long." And the grandkids, they fell in love with it. So I may try restoring it. It's got a little body-work to do to it.

For a while, that was my pleasure truck and my work truck. I worked

with it during the week, and I had to clean it up to go out on weekends. I had the flowers on the borders. That's something we do to attract females. We have our ways.

A pickup — that's a man's vehicle! A car's useful on the weekend, to take the family out, but through the week, you got to have a truck. You can sit high and look down low. Yeah, I miss it. That's why I gotta put it back together. It's been too long.

JAMES MASK

If you catch me sellin' this — boy, my house is gone!

This truck is one thing I don't think I'll ever sell. If you catch me sellin' this—boy, my house is gone!

I went in for back surgery and was out of work for about eight months. It was a miserable time. My wife kept buying books for me and came across this book called *Classic Trucks*. If it weren't for reading that book, and for the back surgery, it may not have ever happened.

I was a mechanic at the time, but I really knew nothing about restoring cars. I bought the truck to learn how to do bodywork. Then I went to get this thing painted after the bodywork was done, and I was told $6,000. You know what kind of books I started reading then—how to paint. So I painted the truck in my garage.

My wife got fed up with me workin' on this thing. She went to bed at 9:30 or so, and as soon as she went to bed, I was in the garage. I came in at two o'clock and went to bed. I got up the next morning and went to work. So 9 to 2 is when this truck got done.

Around 2003, I lost a bunch of money in the stock market and had to pull it out. They gave me a check, and I said, "I'm gonna blow some money on something I couldn't afford to get." I took the little I had left over and spent it on the suspension, the motor, and the transmission. I basically made it into a driver.

What is it about pickups? It's a manly thing. I've always told people this truck has curves like a woman.

LUIS PADILLA

It's one way to express myself and my appreciation for this country.

It was my first vehicle ever. Well, I drove my wife's van in college when we got married. After school, I was ready to get a truck. So that's what I did—a 1998 Dodge Ram with three-inch suspension and big thirty-three-inch tires. Then it went through different stages to get where it is now. I'm still working on a few things. It's legal because the bumper height limit is thirty inches. I'm a half inch below.

In college I didn't do much in politics. In 2007, in the fall,

that's when I got involved in politics. I thought I could use this surface as a way to express myself. I wanted to be part of the Marriage Amendment in 2007, but I didn't have any connection with Republicans or conservative organizations. So I said, "Well, I can use my truck. I can make a big bumper sticker in the back." That got me in trouble, but it gave me good connections. They fired me at work, and then the community came and supported me, and I got my job back.

The truck is a personal expression. Because I'm in this country, I always dream big. I always wanted to have a big truck. I never had a car in my life. Neither did my family. I was born in Honduras. So I wanted to have a big truck as a way to express myself.

People want to know, "Why are you driving a big truck? Why do you have this bumper sticker, this big flag?" So I say, "It's one way to express myself and my appreciation for this country—that now I can call this country my home." My wife and daughters are from this country, so I have a lot of things to attach me here now, after living here for almost twenty years. It's to express my appreciation.

Other people—when they see the bumper stickers—they know my political choice, and they know my social choice. And then they ask, "Are you an American?" Some people wonder if I have the right to have a truck like that.

I enjoy these conversations. It's part of my personality. When someone says, "Nice truck," that gives me an opportunity to have a conversation. Or someone may ask, "Hey, where are you from?" My truck gives me an opportunity to reach out to others. And I get some reactions that are not very appropriate—hand gestures—from people who don't like it. If you don't like it, it's your problem. I don't drive my truck for you to like it. It's a free country.

When I drive on I-81, the tractor trailer drivers, they either give me a thumbs up or they toot the horn. When I see motorcycle guys on Harley-Davidsons with flags in the back, they go crazy. They drive behind me all the way.

It gives a sense of power and confidence. Who's gonna mess with me when I'm drivin' that truck? But

I don't use it that way, even though some people take it that way, and I always respond in a friendly way, even when I get inappropriate reactions. I'm trying to use it as a friendly way to reach out—even to those who think differently.

RON COPELAND

I talk about the economy of the Kingdom with the truck.

My truck is a '91 Toyota. The owner of the Little Grill bought it first. I worked for the Grill, and then when I bought the Grill from him in 1992, I bought the truck, too.

I have this policy that anyone in the world can drive the truck if they have a driver's license and they're not drunk. It was based on the Sermon on the Mount, I guess— just to let people have what they want, if they need it.

People who use it will replace things on it for me and change the oil. I talk about the economy of the Kingdom with the truck. One time there were these folks who were really poor. They didn't have a vehicle, and they wanted to borrow the truck. I said, "Okay, cool," and then it was a couple of days, and a couple of weeks, a month. I didn't really need it, but it was kinda getting irritating. They ended up getting this weird deal where this guy would give them all the metal that was on his land if they would take all the wood off, too.

They ended up bringing nine truckloads of wood to my house, and I heat with wood. So there was enough wood for the whole winter. No one could have predicted that. They didn't have any money; they didn't have any resources. I ended up not having my truck for a little while but then having my heating needs covered and brought right to my house. That's Kingdom economy stuff, where you end up way ahead by just kinda giving it out.

People say to me now, "Hey, Ron, is the community truck available, the hippy truck?" It's kinda gotten out of the consciousness that it's my truck. It just sorta exists. I leave the key in it all the time. It's been stolen a few times. Once this guy who cooked at the Grill's soup kitchen for years and was like a friend took it. Then he wouldn't answer my calls. Months went by. I was like, "Junior, man, you gotta just call me. I don't want the police to be involved." And he wouldn't talk to me. Finally a couple guys from around here, they said, "We're goin' to get it." They just went out and commandeered it. And the guy's wife was chasing after it. He just wasn't givin' it back. It's so bizarre.

It definitely feels like an extension of my person or something. I mean, it feels like— it looks like me. It's blue; it's sorta beat up lookin'. I don't know, I can't explain it. If you look at it closely, it's like Frankenstein—it's always different. A woman took a can of spray paint once and just spray painted all over the door. She painted it solid red with spray paint, though since then the paint chipped off. One door—just solid red. She said, "Look, I painted your truck." I'm like, "Awesome." It's just been that way all along.

The thing about it—because it's a Toyota, it's a great truck. I'd drive it to California and back before I would drive my minivan. Oh, heck, yes. I like to feel like it's protected too or something, but really I think it's Japanese ingenuity.

But yeah, I love it. When I think about possessions that I love, I love my truck and my chain saw. It's ironic, though—I won't loan out my chain saw. It's one thing in the world I won't loan out. But I let everybody use the truck. It seems that's what makes it safe or something. It just reminds me of that commitment to the Sermon on the Mount. Not to use cliché language,

but it has been such a huge blessing to people. If someone doesn't have wheels and needs to get somewhere and someone else just hands them a key, and they don't know them, it shocks people.

People are pretty respectful of it. Everyone knows the key's in it. No one takes it without asking me. Well, except for a few thefts. It would be bad to change my policy with the truck at this point. It's gone so well. What is it, twenty years now? That's something.

I have seen it as a projection of myself, but the truck itself is beyond me. It somehow belongs to everybody. It's really cute. Some people think it's ugly—those who don't know the whole history of it—but I think it's adorable.

TED PELLEGATTA

I have an elm tree growing out of the bed.

It's an '87 Ford F-150 with approximately a half a million miles on it. I bought the truck in '06. Five hundred bucks—that's all I had. And this guy said, "Ted, give me the five and take it, just drive it away." Now I have an elm tree growing out of the bed in the back. It just sprouted.

I started takin' pictures of landscapes after I moved down here. Ever since, it's been a passion; it consumed me. I would be late for deliveries—I'd be stoppin' the truck out there taking pictures. It was like, "You didn't take this picture, Ted." It's still magic to me. The truck is part of my identity now because people have written articles in the paper. It's always, "Ted and his old Ford pickup truck." In fact, it's on the flap of my book of photographs.

About a month ago I was comin' from Charlottesville, a rare bold move to even drive down there. Cop stops me. He comes up to me, and he said, "Do you know why I'm stopping you?" I said, "No sir. I know I wasn't speeding." He said, "You're weavin' all over the road. You been drinkin'?" I said, "Trooper, thirty-four years, I ain't had a drink." He looked at my stickers and said, "United States Marine Corp?" "Yes, sir." "POW-MIA?" "Yes, sir." "Life time membership, NRA?" I said, "That came with the truck. The other stuff is mine." He said I was weavin' all over the place. These old trucks, you got a little play in the steering, so I probably was a little bit.

SUSAN LAING AND VICTORIA LAING

> *The secret of its long life is that it's always been owned by women.*

SUSAN: The truck is a 1990 Toyota. When I bought it, it came with nothing. It had no radio; it had no bumper.

VICTORIA: No power steering, no power brakes.

SUSAN: It's a truck.

VICTORIA: It's a no-kidding truck.

SUSAN: I bought the truck in 1990 and got my dog, Mim, in 1992. Mim loved the truck. I would get the truck out, and she would hop in. We were together for ten years—the truck and Mim and me. When I decided to get a new car in 2002, I thought I would probably sell the truck. Then Mim died, and I thought, "I can't part with my dog and

my truck at the same time." So I held onto the truck.

I used it for running to the dump, and I'd go to church in it. I knew I was supposed to drive it, but I was just not driving it enough. I was thinking of giving it away. And I realized, "My niece, Vic, is getting married, and the man she's marrying doesn't have a car." When I told her, "I'm going to give this to you and Barry as wedding present," she looked at me and said, "When you got married in 1967, you gave me your white horse, Misty." So she's been calling the truck Misty II.

VICTORIA: There was a white horse. Now there's a white truck. It only makes sense.

SUSAN: The culminating part of the story is that the husbands are gone, but we still have the truck!

VICTORIA: Now my son, Karl, wants to know why the truck is sitting in the garage.

SUSAN: Because we have to respect our elders. The tradition here on the farm is that no horses are ever sold or given away. They always die here in the pasture. So Misty II has to spend her last days here on the farm.

VICTORIA: Her last gasp will be here. But I think she's got years left. She doesn't get a whole lot of workout now. She does get to the dump once a week.

SUSAN: The secret of its long life is that it's always been owned by women.

VICTORIA: We don't think we know anything about cars, so we take it in for maintenance.

SUSAN: I don't drive fast, so it's not used to being…

VICTORIA: …hurtled down the road.

SUSAN: For the most part, I'm an easy driver, which is a nice way of saying timid.

VICTORIA: I don't know that it is timid. When we hear about aggressive driving on the news, it's men that they're talking about and not women. I'm not saying that there aren't women that drive aggressively, but I think they're less common. For me, if someone really wants to be in front of me, go ahead!

ROBERT AND MIA STOOP

He's rough and rugged, and the truck is, too.

ROBERT: This is an '01 Chevrolet Silverado I bought for bear huntin'. My wife painted the dog box on it. I've been hunting for about five years now. I went with a friend, and I liked it, so I started buyin' dogs. I've got seven. We average about one bear in a tree a day in December. There's no gun rack because most of us who hunt don't carry guns most of the time. The fun is in the tracking and hearing the dogs. If we don't have weapons, we can track the dogs onto private property.

MIA: The dogs know what that truck is—they do. As soon as we start that truck up,

this one here in the front just goes nuts. They have their own spots in the truck. And when they're hunting, it's amazing how I can be up there and pick out our set of dogs; from each bark I can tell who's who. It's amazing how far they'll travel, though.

I married into bear hunting. At first I wasn't sure about it. But once I went, I loved it. It's not so much the hunting as it is being in the mountains, being with the dogs, being with him. It's just a whole new world up there. Everybody is up on the mountain, and we can hear everybody talkin' and stuff. And to know that he's out there chasin' the dogs,

tracking the dogs down—it's pretty wild. I usually sit in the truck and draw. And I take tons of pictures. I'm the designated driver. They do all the walkin', and I do all the drivin'.

I would say the truck is like him because he's constantly on the move. He's rough and rugged, and the truck is, too. He has no fear with that truck. He gets in it and does whatever. It's like a tank to him.

H.R. COMPTON

I've got too many toys for what I do.

I just have these two nice vintage pickups. I'm a Chevy man—you can tell that, can't you? I always liked Chevys. My daddy was a Chevy man. And I also got into antique tractors. I just kept buying tractors.

I got 'bout sixty of 'em. I've got too many toys for what I do. But I just like that old stuff.

The '49 ain't all original. The body is, but the runnin' gear ain't. It's two tone—burgundy and red. I like that. They call this the "five windows," but it's got more than five windows. I don't know why they call it five windows. It's quite a decent little truck.

The other is a '72. A mechanic sold it to a friend of mine. His son

got in trouble, and he needed the money, so he sold it to me. I just like the body style. They drive good, and it's easy to get in and out.

I take them out to parades, but I just wish I had more time. My wife says, "Why don't you retire?" I just turned 68 years old, but I like to get out and work—work with people and all. I just don't wanta sit around.

I bought this little old 2½ horsepower engine at a flea market. It's what they used in the mines to pull. I put it in this truck. I put it in parades and car shows, and I have gotten trophies just 'cause I had this sittin' in the back. It's unusual.

BROOKE RODGERS

> ## *If people drop the ego thing, they can learn a lot.*

I bought this truck with no transmission. I'd been looking for something that I could throw plywood and gear into. I was bartending at the American Legion. There I've met guys who know how to do pretty much everything, and they love teaching. One of them, Butch, was a car person. Butch said, "There's a waterman* friend of mine who's got a truck. The transmission needs to be replaced, so the price is really cheap, and we can do it together." I love doin' stuff like that, and he has a whole shop.

So I got the truck. We got a transmission out of a junk truck, and I got to put the whole thing in. He told me what to do, and he has every tool in the whole world. I took more pictures than anyone will ever want to look at.

* People who make a living by fishing, crabbing, and oystering on the Chesapeake Bay are called waterman.

By the time we got it running, I pretty much wanted to take apart everything else in it because I learned so much. It turns out that if you have small hands, it's good. And I call Butch every time something goes wrong with it. He helps me figure out what it is. The other day it was killing the battery, and we decided that it was the ignition. Butch called me before he went off on a three-day vacation to make sure everything was good. He was allowed to go out of town and not be there to come to my rescue with his tools.

I use the truck for pretty much everything. I use it for moving around beehives. I had it filled with plywood the other day for building a wall. The toolbox is usually full of my beekeeping gear, jumper cables, and my diving weight belt. Usually the back has a bucket full of pine needles for the smoker and then dive gear. I was a scientific diver in grad school, and so I do whatever people need done under water. I have so many student loans that I'm willing to do a little bit of everything. When I was looking for work after grad school, I was looking for something in the sciences, but I recognized that my jack-of-all-trades background is actually my biggest selling point—whatever you need.

It probably helps to be a young woman. It also helps that everybody knows I have every hobby and interest in the world. If anybody has a tool, they say, "We've got a jointer. Do you want it?" "Yeah. I need to own that." My shop is completely crammed with tools.

Being a girl helps with all that kinda stuff because I'm pretty good at being grossly incompetent at things. I'm actually a very competent person, but I don't mind being a total beginner and saying, "I'm really interested in this, but I don't know anything. What's a carburetor?" I'm pretty good at picking things up quickly, which people who like teaching tend to find

enjoyable. They're willing to have me around because I'm willing to work hard and not get paid as long as I get to learn about something. If people drop the ego thing, they can learn a lot. Yeah, people can have all kinds of wild experiences on the Shore if they're willing to be interested in anything.

When I had just finished art school, I had a little bit of money, and I decided the best idea was to get a pickup with a roll bar. So I bought it from this kid in Rhode Island who clearly assembled it from random things he found in his yard. I had it in Boston for a while, and it broke down from the moment I bought it.

I decided to go on a road trip, since it was already breaking down, and clearly that makes the most sense at age 21 or 22—driving around alone. I got fifty miles out of Boston before it broke down the first time. I made it to North Carolina, and a guy there helped me work on it. We revived it, and then I made it to Lexington, Kentucky, where my friends were living. And then as I was heading back to Boston, the truck completely blew up in Hurricane, West Virginia. I sold it for fifty bucks and a ride back to the hotel. I got my friends to pick me up, and I moved to Kentucky. So that was my first pickup.

From Brooke's business card:

Scientific diving, sewing and embroidery, experimental design and construction, small boat operation, beer brewing, cheese making, sailing, scrimshaw, taxidermy, stained glass, turtle husbandry, data management and analysis, basic plumbing, mesocosm setup and operation, YSI & CTD, Diving PAM fluorometry, bike repair, gardening, drawing, stone masonry, problem solving, design, and intervention.

LARRY ARMSTRONG AND JENNIFER ARMSTRONG

It's titled as a '46 F1, but it's got probably eight or ten vehicles in it.

It's titled as '46 F1, but it's got probably eight or ten different vehicles in it. And a lot of hand-made parts. Some people think this is an unsafe ride, but it's not because everything that's important is brand new: frame, suspension, brakes. It's just made to look old. All the cosmetics are old.

The cars at the show here are beautiful, but a lot of people don't build their cars. They buy 'em. Or they have somebody else restore 'em. There are only a few people who build 'em. I did everything on this that I could. There are beautiful cars around here, but they require high maintenance. With mine, it doesn't matter. I still got mud on it from when I ran it on the dirt track last year.

JENN (DAUGHTER): I drove it for the first time a few weeks ago. There's no power steering so that was interesting. I had to use all my muscle. It's fun though.

MIKE ZOOK

I'm not that stereotype of a guy who just needed a truck.

I'm not that stereotype of a guy who just needed a truck. They're definitely convenient for a lot of things, but I mainly got a truck because of my landscaping work. And it's convenient if I do get a deer. I don't want to be puttin' that in the back of a station wagon. So this is my hunting and work truck.

I think people who tend to drive trucks like this are a little bit macho, and I don't feel like that's me. So I don't think the truck says much about me. I like things to be pretty neat and stuff, and with my truck being a work truck, there's no sense in washing it or anything like that. It has a few little dents, a few squeaks, and broken parts.

I got into bow hunting, and that's my true passion. It's not as cold during bow hunting, and I think it's more of a challenge. There are different levels of hunters. Some people just want to kill; some people hunt to get meat. I just enjoy being outdoors. I don't necessarily need to shoot something to have a successful hunt.

My license plate is Buck Fever, but it's spelled BUCPHVR. My dad has BUKFEVR. I tried to get BUCFEVR, but it was already taken.

COREY OMPS

I like horsepower.

This is a pullin' truck. It's built for sled pullin'. We just built it this winter, and we're gonna run it tonight. It's something new. Pretty much everything's redone. You name it, it's been touched.

I took the original engine out and put a 12-valve Cummins in there. I didn't go the automatic transmission route because there's a pile of money in transmissions. On a manual transmission, all I have to have is a good clutch, and I'm good to go. At least that's what I think. I'll find out. We ran it

earlier today, and everything worked pretty good, so it should work out just fine.

I guess I'm like everybody else—I like horsepower.

DAVID BURDEN

It's like seeing somebody else out to dinner with your girlfriend.

This is the only new vehicle I've owned. I spent a lot of time looking, and I got the perfect truck for what I do. I am certainly not easy on things, and it has earned its keep.

My business does kayaks, kite boarding, and standup paddle boarding. Lessons, trips, rentals, and sales—different boats for different folks. I also work for a nonprofit water quality advocacy group. So I tow my boat with it

and pull around a trailer loaded with paddle boards, kayaks, kite boarding gear, bikes, and dogs. It just does everything. It's been an awesome truck. I lived out of it driving to the Keys and back, sellin' boats on the road. It's been everywhere.

I recently blew up the engine. Everybody was pretty much saying, "Hey, it's scrap metal now," but honestly, I'm gonna put a new engine in it 'cause I think it's a great truck. It's nothin' fancy—rollup windows, broken CD player. I was explaining it to my friend who asked, "Why don't you just get a different truck?" I know this truck! This truck knows how to live with me. I know how to load it, I know what it can take, and it'll hang in there. I abused it a little too much and pushed it a little bit too far, but now I know its limitations.

It's a little Dodge Dakota. It's not designed to be a big burley work truck, but I treat it like it's one. It's sorta the combination of the utility of having a small truck and the utility of having a big truck all wrapped into one.

You get attached to certain vehicles, and they become not animate but important. I've woken up in that truck with the tires in the sand on the beach in Florida. It's been on a number of adventures from surf-ing to paddling. Throw a couple of these chairs in the back, park it on the beach backwards, and watch the sunset. Honestly, there are weeks in the summer when I spend more time in that truck than I spend at home. So it sorta feels like home.

I think if someone parked ten vehicles in a line and pulled me and nine other people together, everyone would know that I belong with that vehicle. It's dirty, it's beat up, and it's got a bunch of beach toys in it. And that's sorta me. There's always sand on the windshield; there's always some kind of toys in it; there's usually a little bit of yesterday's lunch still in the cooler and maybe a cold beer for the sunset somewhere in the back as well.

I've killed four other vehicles while I've had that truck. And it's been my primary vehicle that whole time. So yeah, I'm hard on trucks. This one's a gem. It doesn't define me, but it identifies well with my lifestyle.

People will call me and say, "Man I saw someone else driving your truck. What's goin' on?" It's not even, "I'm worried that someone stole your truck," but, "Man, seein' someone else in your truck is really weird. It's like seeing someone else out to dinner with your girlfriend."

RICHARD RANDOLPH

> *It's a real joy that it can be as old as it is and still be useful.*

I wanted to be a truck driver since I was 9 years old. My daddy bought me a toy truck for my ninth Christmas. It was beautiful. And I lay down on the floor and played with it. I could back that little trailer up.

Then the first time I ever got in a trailer truck in my life was in the military. They put me on guard duty out at the airport, and I would take the tankers and drive around the airport and then see if I could put 'em back where they were, at night, in the dark. And I could do it. Finally I got caught by a sergeant, and he said, "I'm not gonna tell on you. You outta put in for trailer driving." So I went on and did that.

Me and my dad had our own truck. Best compliment

I got in my life was when my daddy told me, "You're the best truck driver I've seen." Course, you know there's a lot of bias in that, but he did teach driving in the military. And that was a real honor for me.

I had security clearance for thirty years. I drove trucks to all the government buildings—the Pentagon, any of those, I'd go into them. But the White House was the main place they wanted me to go. Once I was at the Rose Garden, and I banged the tailgate. Out came the guns—machine guns. They were all around the White House. They said, "You know you made George Bush change his under-clothes with that noise? Don't do that no more when you come in here." "Yes sir, I won't do that no more."

Gorbachev, the Russian premier, was at the White House one time. I came in there, and—talk about clean—I had the Mac truck cleaned that day. He waved at me, gave me the okay signal.

As much as I love trucks, I was in my forties before I bought a pickup truck. It was a Ford Ranchero. Oh, was that thing ugly. I had a 400 cubic inch motor in it, and it was fast, but it was ugly.

I always wanted an El Camino. When I got to where I had all this arthritis and was retired and had a heart attack, I didn't want a great big old truck. So I went lookin' for one of them. It took awhile, but I found her.

And I liked the color. It's one of the prettier ones. It's a Super Sport, for one thing—an '84. I just fell in love with it. I like that it's a truck, but it's not a cumbersome truck. I had gotten out of big trucks, and I didn't need a big truck. It's a real joy that it can be as old as it is and still be useful.

I use it. I've had people walk up to me and say it was a shame that I had a load on it. I said, "Well, it's not doin' me no good if I don't."

Somebody's been takin' care of it; it's got a few more years left in it. I use it as if I was using a regular truck. It's hard on gas but got a lot of power. It doesn't have but a 305 and a 4-barrel, but it's an electronic 4-barrel. If I would get out there and try to race, it won't open up. But if I put weight on it, it will. I wouldn't trade it for nothin'.

Let me tell you about Boonsboro. There was a Klu Klux Klan parade there. That was when they could wear their hoods—about twenty-five years ago. I came to the tail end of the parade. I didn't know what was goin' on. I was in a red International Scout with a red trailer and a red Farmall tractor up on the back of it. And I was wearing an International hat. This guy stopped me. He said, "Parade ahead of us. You have to wait until this goes through before I let you through. Where you goin'?"

I said, "Down the street about six blocks, then make a right." He said, "When I get a break, toward the end of it, I'll let you in because I ain't never seen a black man set up like you are. You can't be but so bad!" And I said, "No, I'm not bad at all." He let me into the end of the Klu Klux Klan parade. Here I came down the street, lookin' like I was in the parade. That was me and the Klan.

RANDY GREEN

Every time I get in the truck, it's like he's riding with me.

This truck is a '49 GMC and has been in my family. My grandfather was living in St. Maries, Idaho, and had started a dealership there. This was the first truck that he ordered from GMC—for his brother-in-law, Ed. It's got the extra cab, the demountable wheels. They ordered some special stuff with it like the radio options.

Ed had a service station in Klamath Falls, Oregon, and so he used it around there. I have his calendar for his service station. He wrote on June 24, 1949, to pick it up in Oakland, California. That's the only thing written in there. I saw what was important to him! I think Ed passed away in '79, so my grandfather took it and had it at his hardware store in Shady Cove, Oregon. I remember as a kid going a couple places with him in it. Then they moved back to Idaho, and it stayed there until about '88 or '89, when they had to move. He couldn't take the truck, so my dad called me and said, "He wants you to have it."

I spent the next ten years or so restoring it. The bed was really beat up 'cause they hauled wood, and they hunted. The bed took me the most time to try to get straight. All the sheet metal that's in it is pretty much what it was; nothing has been replaced. I wanted to keep the original sheet metal on it. The engine is original—I never even rebuilt it. Grandpa maintained it, and Ed maintained it. I never rebuilt the transmission either. I did the suspension, of course, and the brakes.

That bumper was something that Ed made up. I mean, they're frickin' loggers out there. They didn't do things light. I debated on cutting it off, but finally I just decided, "I'm gonna leave it. It's part of the truck, man." And although you can buy new glove boxes for these trucks, my grandfather had done some work on it. It ain't the greatest, but I said, "I'm not gonna buy a new glove box. It's a piece of history." It sounds sentimental, but it's little things like that I think of when I'm riding around in it. Every time I get in the truck, it's like he's riding with me.

To me, more than anything, it is about people. My grandfather and I were always separated. When I was doing the truck, it allowed us to be in touch. Even though I knew what was going on, I'd act like I didn't sometimes, and it opened up a correspondence between us. I sent 'im a ton of pictures as I was building it, and it just opened up something between us that was important to both of us. He was involved, and I think that was the biggest blessing for me.

I've hit some hard times, and I thought I needed to sell it one time. My daughter had just moved here, and I was the only one taking care of her. She's got cerebral palsy. I was like, "Man, I don't have any money, so I'm gonna sell it." I took it down to the drag strip, to a super Chevy event. Those guys had all these drag cars on their trailers, and here I was with the little pickup. The guys asked, "Man, what's the story with that truck?" And then after they heard the story, they said, "Man, you can't sell that truck. What's wrong with you?!" So these strangers—I said, "They're right! I can't sell this truck!" I'm grateful that I have it.

My daughter and I have had fun in it. And when anybody comes, like my sister, we gotta get it out and ride around. I'm sure the rest of society doesn't like it very much. It takes a while to get away from the stop sign, to get in the next gear. And 55 is all it wants to do. People are so impatient. That's kinda why I don't drive it that much anymore. It takes some of the fun out of it. You get people honkin' at you. You don't wanta go around flippin' everybody off. But I like to take it out some on the holidays when there's less traffic and have some fun.

RICH BRYAN

> *Neither of us is ready to give up,*
> *but I can see the end coming.*
> *Which of us is going first?*

I never thought I'd be in competition with my Ford pickup truck. But the more I thought of the similarities, the more similarities I came up with.

We are both old and both retired. I'm 75, and my truck is a 1995 F-150—old in truck years. I'm a bricklayer and used it right good carrying loads on construction sites. Each of us has a lot of miles on us. My truck has 436,000 miles on it, and I have been married

over fifty years. We both could use a tune-up and some repair. We did get some new parts. We both got our rear ends worked on.

That pickup is part of me, I guess. I have a little chair out at the shed, and I go out there and sit and keep the truck company. We keep each other company now.

Neither of us is ready to give up, but I can see the end coming. Which of us is going first? Right now it's a dead heat.

PICKUPS, THE HISTORY OF A LOVE STORY

Essay by Mark Metzler Sawin

Perhaps a book about people and their pickup trucks seems like an odd topic. After all, almost all Americans own vehicles—it's just a necessary part of life in most of the United States. It seems that a book about people and their trucks would be about the same as a book about people and their toasters, or people and their washing machines. Most people own those things, too. But all machinery is not equal. People are attached to some of their things far more than to others. Few people are passionate about their blenders or vacuum cleaners. But their pickup trucks—that's another matter.

The idea behind this book was simple. Howard Zehr decided to talk to as many folks as he could about their pickups: men and women, old and young, rich and poor, city and country, black, brown, and white. What he found was an amazing set of profound and unique stories. But even though every story is different, in one way they're all the same. These people love their trucks. They name them, care for them, lavish attention on them, and treat them like members of the family. Their trucks represent the stories of their lives—they explain their pasts, presents, and futures, their fears and ambitions, hopes and dreams.

What we have here, then, are various "love stories" about many different people and their pickups. After helping Howard with this project (he let me tag along on several of his interviewing adventures), I began to wonder about the bigger story—the story of the U.S.'s love affair with this distinctly American machine. The more of these stories I heard, the more curious I became, so I decided to investigate this American romance with the pickup. Here's what I found.

Beginning in the mid-1970s, Americans went on a pickup truck bender. They started buying more pick-ups than ever, and this spree has kept right on going ever since. In 1999, for the first time in U.S. history, Americans bought more new trucks than cars, and since 1999, new pickup sales have remained ahead of car sales in ten out of twelve years. Americans aren't buying just a few more trucks than cars; they're buying a lot more trucks! In many recent years, trucks have out-sold cars by double-digit percentages and millions of total sales.

This American obsession with pickups was in many ways a patriotic act because it largely saved the U.S. auto industry. Since the 1980s, foreign manufacturers have gobbled up more and more of the U.S. auto market. During this same time, U.S. manufacturers turned increasingly to pickups to balance their bottom lines. In 1998, U.S. manufacturers made more trucks than cars for the first time, and since 2000, U.S. manufacturers have typically made between ten percent and twenty percent more trucks than cars. To put this in perspective, it's worth noting that since 2000, U.S. manufacturers have produced more than 83 million trucks. That's roughly one for every four people living in the United States—enough for one truck for every American family.[1]

Americans love trucks. That is not a question but a fact. But the reason why they love them is worth digging into a bit further. This very question often strikes visitors to the United States because in most other parts of the globe (with the exceptions of Australia, Canada, and Mexico, where pickups are also common), few people buy pickups. As one baffled Dutch immigrant explained to his old-world friends, "A pickup truck is basically a larger version of a car that comes with a bouncy ride, less comforts, uses considerably more gas, and is harder to park." Despite these issues, however, he was surprised to find that every "real American family" has one.[2]

As the stories in this book show, there are as many different reasons for owning a pickup as there are people who own them, but there do seem to be some themes that explain America's truck love affair. Pickups seem to represent the American character itself: individualism, self-reliance, freedom, and a "pursuit of happiness." When Thomas Jefferson penned the Declaration of Independence, he proclaimed the inalienable rights of life, liberty, and the pursuit of happiness. In this way, Jefferson was getting at an important idea: People are defined not only by who they are but also by the things they own—the things they use to earn their living, take care of their family, and pursue their happiness. Given this idea, Americans' love of trucks starts to become clearer. Pickup trucks are tools that many people use in their daily lives, but even more importantly, they are an important part of people's pursuit of happiness.

Pickup trucks first emerged after WWI when Dodge, Chevrolet, and Ford all began producing small trucks for civilian use. In 1925, Ford offered an alternative body to its famous Model T, calling the option a "Runabout with Pickup Body" and thus coining the term "pickup."[3] The vehicles were made to work and to navigate unpaved roads. (Just over one percent of America's three million miles of roads were paved in 1920.) They were vehicles for country folk and for farm work. According to the U.S. Department of Agriculture, in 1920 there were more than 6.5 million farms in America, and nearly half of all Americans lived in the country with 13.5 million people (one fourth of all workers) doing some sort of farming. These numbers stayed about the same for the next several decades, but following WWII, the number of

American farmers began to drop sharply as more and more people moved to urban and suburban areas, pulled there by factory and service jobs. By the 1970s, more than four million farms had disappeared, and the number of people working in agriculture had dropped by two-thirds.[4]

With this huge shift away from rural life and farming, it would have made sense for pickup truck sales to go down. Far fewer people lived on farms and needed trucks for their daily work. But that's not what happened. In fact, it was just the reverse. Pickup sales boomed.

Why this happened is an interesting question, and one that doesn't have any easy answers, because at face value it doesn't make sense. Why would people buy more trucks when they actually needed them less? After all, people living in towns and working in factories or shops don't need to haul hay or livestock; they don't need to drive over washboard country roads or pull heavy equipment. But perhaps that's the wrong way to look at it, because pickups aren't just about what they can do. They're also about what they mean—they're about the pursuit of happiness.

When Americans farmed, they were largely dependent on themselves. Their success was built on their own hard work, ingenuity, and ability to get things done. The ideal American farmer is representative of the American ideal itself. Farmers are people who plant their own crops, build their own buildings, raise their own food, fix their own equipment, and succeed or fail

because of the might of their own arms, the sweat of their brows, and the cleverness of their minds. They are "real Americans"—the kind who settled the frontier, tamed the Wild West, surrounded their houses with picket fences, baked apple pies, and didn't owe anything to anyone.

But this ideal rural, free, American lifestyle just wasn't how most Americans lived by the 1970s, and it's not how most of us live now. It's also true that most Americans today do not want to trade their new homes and 8 to 5 jobs for the hard work and long hours of the rural farmer. However, that does not mean that Americans don't still idealize that up-by-the-bootstraps country lifestyle. It's not surprising, then, that many Americans, despite their "modern" lives, seek to keep the trappings of the rural, rugged, independent life of America's earlier farming and frontier societies.

This becomes quite clear when you look at the late 1970s and early 1980s. At that time, more Americans were living in cities and doing shift-work jobs, but they were still longing for the freedom of the country life. At that same time, country music became far more popular as singers like Kenny Rogers, Dolly Parton, and John Denver all scored cross-over hits on pop-music charts. Stetson hats, belt buckles, and country fashion became mainstream, and films like John Travolta's *Urban Cowboy* did very well at the box office. And pickup truck sales boomed! Today some of these trends have left us (country music remains very popular; big belt buckles less so), but pickup trucks have remained a potent symbol of this country ideal. And their sales have continued to expand: 12 million pickups were sold in the 1960s; 29 million in the 1970s; 40 million in the 1980s; 64 million in the 1990s; and a whopping 86 million in the 2000s.[5]

A quick look at some current pickup truck names shows the continued rugged and rural understanding of this vehicle: Silverado, Ridgeline, Sierra, Ram, Tundra, Frontier, Colorado, Dakota, Canyon, and Ranger. These are names that project images of the frontier and the farm and of an era of rugged individualism—an image that still clearly appeals to many Americans.

As the stories in this book portray, the ideas of independence and self-sufficiency are alive and well in the hearts of many pickup owners. However, it is also clear that for many folks such ideas have little or nothing to do with why they have and love a truck. Love is a complicated thing. Trucks tie people to their pasts and represent fresh starts. They show strong family connections and mark breaks in relationships. Trucks represent freedom and individualism for some, but for others, trucks tie them closely to a community and represent the unity of small-town life. Some folks proudly baby their trucks, keeping them spotlessly clean and glowingly shined; others proudly abuse them, feeling they aren't "real" until they're a bit beaten up around the edges. Pickups are used for work, for commuting, for show, for competitions, and for status.

In the end, however, one thing is abundantly clear. Regardless of who owns them, what they are used for, when they were made, where they call home, or how they fit into people's lives, the reason people own trucks is always clear. It's because they love them. And in the end, that's all that really matters.

— Mark Metzler Sawin is Professor of History at Eastern Mennonite University. He drives a thirty-year-old Mercedes station wagon that he has nursed along for more than 333,333 miles.

[1] "U.S. Vehicle Sales, 1931-2011" and "North American Car and Truck Production, 1951-2011," WardsAuto, The Information Center for and about the Global Auto Industry, http://wardsauto.com/keydata/historical/UsaSa01summary; and 2010 U.S. Census Data, http://2010.census.gov/2010census/data/.

[2] Niek Smit, "Explaining Pickups to Foreigners and Immigrants," Jalopnik.com, Oct. 3, 2010, http://jalopnik.com/5654507/.

[3] The best, easy-to-access history of the pickup is Don Bunn and Paul McLaughlin, "A History of the American Pickup Truck," PickupTrucks.com, http://www.pickuptrucks.com/html/history/history.html.

[4] "U.S. Number of Farms and All Farm Workers," United States Department of Agriculture National Agriculture Statistics Survey, http://www.nass.usda.gov/Charts_and_Maps/Farm_Labor/fl_frmwk.asp; and Tiffiney Carney, "Paving the Way," Route 66: The main stream of America, University of Virginia XRoads project, http://xroads.virginia.edu/~ug02/carney/paving.html.

[5] "U.S. Vehicle Sales, 1931-2011," WardsAuto.

3 1901 05409 5239

ABOUT THE AUTHOR AND PHOTOGRAP

Howard Zehr is internationally known for his leadership in the field of restorative justice. However, for many years he also worked part time as a photographer and has traveled in many countries as a photojournalist. His books about or containing photography include *The Little Book of Contemplative Photography*; *Doing Life: Reflections of Men and Woman Serving Life Sentences*; *Transcending: Reflections of Crime Victims*; and *What Will Happen to Me?* (about children whose parents are in prison), all published by Good Books. Some of his personal photography may be viewed at www.howardzehr.com.

Zehr received his B.A. from Morehouse College and his Ph.D. in history from Rutgers University. He is Distinguished Professor of Restorative Justice at the Center for Justice and Peacebuilding, Eastern Mennonite University, Harrisonburg, Virginia. His current photogr interests include landscapes, portraits, and documentary projects.

3 1901 05409 5239